Mastermind

Mastermind

questions and answers from the BBC tv quiz game
compiled by Boswell Taylor

British Broadcasting Corporation

Published by the British Broadcasting Corporation,
35 Marylebone High Street, London W1M 4AA

ISBN 0 563 12570 5

First published 1973

Printed in England by Hunt Barnard Printing Ltd,
Aylesbury, Bucks

Contents

Introduction

Most good ideas are invariably simple ones, and I think this is the strength of *Mastermind*. Devoid of all the usual quiz gimmickery it is a simple confrontation of Questioner and Questioned.

How did it all begin? It began in the Quiz Unit office of the Entertainment Department of Outside Broadcasts – a unit that has been responsible for *Television Top of the Form*, *Quiz Ball* and *Transworld Top Team*. We produced also a television version of *Brain of Britain* some years ago, but I had always thought that television ought to be able to produce an intellectual quiz that was entirely original. *Mastermind* gradually took shape from the basic concept of a single contestant with an interrogator firing questions. Many titles were considered but the name Mastermind, an inspiration of *Television Top of the Form* researcher Mary Craig, was eventually decided on.

Luck of course plays a part in any competition and *Mastermind* is no exception, but I think we have achieved with this format a competition that reduces the luck factor to a minimum. To qualify as *Mastermind* material you have to know your chosen subject thoroughly to stand any sort of chance at all. Couple the degree of excellence in a given subject with a sharp, decisive and concise mind and you have the qualifications required to enter for the title 'Mastermind of the United Kingdom'.

Any television programme, simple or otherwise, requires a great deal of team work, and I would like to pay tribute to my production team, particularly Martin Bell our director, Cherry Cole our hard-working researcher, Janet Evans who is now without doubt the most informed typist in the business, and Philip Lindley our designer; to my engineering colleagues and, of course, the star of the show, Magnus Magnusson who has so adroitly developed an art of gentle interrogation. This team has worked hard together to make the series a success.

Bill Wright, Executive Producer

General Knowledge 1

1 Who designed the 'bouncing bomb' used by the 'Dam Busters' to destroy the Ruhr dams in World War II?

2 What is the name of the bell used at Lloyd's in London?

3 In what year did Mussolini invade Ethiopia?

4 Which group of people were emancipated in Britain in 1829?

5 At one time a member of Diaghilev's Company, she became Director of the Royal Ballet. Who is she?

6 He was the author of *The Shortest Way with Dissenters* and *A Journal of the Plague Year*. Who was he?

7 The Roman goddess of agriculture who bore a daughter by Jupiter is identified with the Greek goddess Demeter. What is her name?

8 What are the names of the two large towers of the Palace of Westminster?

9 Who was the founder of the German 'Christian Democratic Party'?

10 Which (contemporary) composer first used the Dodecaphonic Scale in his later works?

11 The yield of an oil well is measured in barrels. How many gallons are there to a barrel?

12 What special gift did Jean Baptiste Tavernier present to King Louis XIV of France?

13 Why do Tibetan priests search for a boy after the death of the Dalai Lama?

14 In what part of the world would you find a Gamelan Orchestra?

15 His first play was *The Room* in 1957 and his other works include *The Servant*. What is his name?

16 What is natation?

17 What is the name of the Rake in *The Rake's Progress*?

18 In the theatre, what would you be doing if you were 'papering the house'?

19 Goethe wrote about him; Berlioz, Wagner and Liszt all composed music about him. Who was he?

20 What is the capital of Nepal?

Twentieth-century English Literature
Set by Boswell Taylor

21　What book, modelled on Homer's *Odyssey*, tells the story of a day in Dublin?

22　*Man of Property* is the first book in Galsworthy's trilogy *Forsyte Saga*, what is the last?

23　What is the name of the large island which is the setting for Conrad's *Almayer's Folly* and *An Outcast of the Islands*?

24　D. H. Lawrence adopted the phoenix as a personal symbol. What bird is named in the title of his first novel?

25　What twentieth-century novel has as its epigraph the words 'only connect . . .'?

26　Alec Waugh, brother of Evelyn, wrote a first novel about life at a public school, what was it?

27　What is the connection between Lady Ariadne Utterwood and Mrs Hesione Hushabye?

28　Which modern novel ends with the words 'She walked rapidly in the June sunlight towards the worst horror of all'?

29　Who was the predecessor of Cecil Day-Lewis as Poet Laureate?

30　What poet wrote this epitaph for his own grave: 'cast a cold eye, on life, on death. Horseman, pass by!'?

31　How did Edward Ponderevo make his fortune?

32　What is the title of Shaw's five-part play which is supposed to trace the entire history of mankind?

33 Where do you find Willy Nilly, Organ Morgan and Bessie Bighead?

34 Justine, Balthazar, Mountolive, what's the fourth?

35 What is the real name of the British Intelligence Officer who created *The Spy who Came in from the Cold*?

36 What is the title of the book published in 1954, which is a black parody of Ballantyne's *Coral Island*?

37 What were the first names of Dame Edith Sitwell's famous brothers?

38 Who wrote the wartime book *The Last Enemy*?

39 Who were Priestley's 'Good Companions'?

40 What is the name of the Tibetan mountain retreat described by James Hilton in *The Lost Horizon*?

National Flags Past and Present
Set by I. O. Evans

41 What flags were raised above the summit of Mount Everest by Hillary and Tensing in 1953?

42 We all know the Stars and Stripes, but what were the Stars and Bars?

43 What emblems are used, and where, for the Red Cross Flag?

44 How many stripes appear on the National Flag of Greece, and why?

45 What is the translation of the Arabic script on the flag of Saudi Arabia?

46 Explain how a certain national flag was inspired by an Aztec legend.

47 Which was the first flag to reach the Moon?

48 Which flag of a foreign region resembles a British Ensign in having the so-called Union Jack in its canton and what is the design on the remainder of the flag?

49 What were the colours of the original flag of the Netherlands and why were they varied?

50 What flag bears a representation of St George slaying the Dragon?

51 How is the State Flag of East Germany distinguished from the National Flag of West Germany?

52 What two National Flags display the 'Sun of May' and why?

53 Which two flags were the first to reach the South Pole?

54 How are the flags of the constituent Republics of the Soviet Union distinguished from that of the Soviet Union itself?

55 What foreign flag most resembles the British Union Flag and in what respects does it differ from this?

56 The flags of what regions bear emblems of the rising or the setting sun, and why was the latter chosen?

57 What emblem appeared on the American flag flown at the Battle of Concord and what historic British flag does it resemble?

58 Why were the Lilies of France shown in the place of honour in the English Royal Standard?

59 What former National Flag is now used as the House Flag of a shipping line?

60 What is, or was, the Sabah Jack?

IDRISYN OLIVER EVANS: author of *The Observer's Book of Flags* (Warne), and *The Book of Flags* (OUP).

General Knowledge 2

61 He directed *Rembrandt* and *Lady Hamilton* and produced *The Scarlet Pimpernel* and *The Third Man*. Who was he?

62 James I of England presided over an important conference held at Hampton Court in 1604. What did it bring about?

63 What mythological creature was half-man and half-horse?

64 Originally a French eighteenth-century innovation, what is the method of gilding furniture and clocks known as?

65 Rigel and Betelgeuse are two stars in which constellation?

66 Who was the world's first woman Prime Minister?

67 The Adi Granth is a holy book of which religion?

68 What was the sensational discovery of Charles Dawson in Sussex in the early years of the present century?

69 What famous building was built at Alexandria in the region of Ptolemy (308-245 BC)?

70 Ouagadougou is the capital of which country?

71 How many women's colleges are there in Oxford University?

72 Who said: 'Let us never negotiate out of fear. But let us never fear to negotiate.'?

73 King Edward III founded this premier Order in about 1349. What is it called?

74 What is 'The Witch of Wookey'?

75 Of which Canadian Party is Pierre Trudeau the leader?

76 He first came to Europe from America in 1857 and amongst his most famous paintings is a portrait of his mother. Who was he?

77 A village in Huntingdonshire is famous for its cheese. What is its name?

78 In Greek Legend who was Pygmalion?

79 What is majolica?

80 What is the largest organ in the human body?

Grand Opera

Set by Harold Rosenthal

81 What is the English translation of the title of the opera 'Die Verkaufte Braut'?

82 Who composed the opera 'Oedipus Rex'?

83 What does the word 'Opera' mean?

84 From which author's story was the opera 'Barber of Seville' taken?

85 Mussorgsky's 'Boris Godunov' was based on a play by whom?

86 Where was 'Das Rheingold' first performed?

87 Who was Helen Mitchell?

88 The songs 'Once there lived a king in Thule' and 'Forever Thine' come from which opera?

89 Name the first opera ever performed.

90 Where was the first public opera house opened?

91 What famous opera house stands on the site of a church?

92 How many Rossini operas have the same overture?

93 How many conquests did Don Giovanni make in Spain, according to Leporello's cataloguing?

94 When audiences acclaimed Verdi with the shouts 'Viva Verdi' what political significance did these words have?

95 How many Walküres were there?

96 What was the 'mystic gulf'?

97 Who was Uncle Greifenklau?

98 What famous opera takes place while another opera is supposed to be played off stage?

99 By what name is June Gough better known?

100 Who was Gualtier Malde?

HAROLD ROSENTHAL: Editor of *Opera*, writer on music, formerly archivist at the Royal Opera House, Covent Garden.

Astronomy 1

Set by Patrick Moore

101 Which planet was discovered in 1930?

102 What is the Cassini division?

103 What would happen to the moon of a planet if it passed the Roche limit?

104 The Trojans are groups of asteroids that move in the same orbit as one of the planets. Which planet?

105 How many moons has Saturn?

106 Mercury orbits the Sun once every 88 days. How long does it take for Mercury to rotate once on its axis?

107 What is a pulsar?

108 What planet is known as the Horned Planet?

109 Who discovered the planet Uranus?

110 Which planet has the least density?

111 For what was Flamsteed famous?

112 Fred Hoyle put forward a theory of creation. What did he call it?

113 Where, today, would you expect to find Hell, Julius Caesar, Birmingham, Billy, Ptolemaeus and Archimedes?

114 On 25 October 1973 the planet Mars will be at opposition. What precisely does this mean?

115 What was the name of the great Dutch astronomer who discovered a supernova in 1572 and who drew up a famous star catalogue?

116 The lunar craters, Gassendi, Hippalus, Doppelmayer, Vitello and Lee lie around the border of a well-defined sea or Mare. Name the Mare.

117 Only three external galaxies are clearly visible with the naked eye. Which of them can be seen from the latitude of London?

118 What is the significance of the apparently chaotic sequence of letters W, O, B, A, F, G, K, M?

119 What is particular about the orbit of Pluto?

120 Of the following ten stars, nine are long-period variables and the tenth is irregular. Name the irregular variables from: W Lyrae, R Leonis, R Arietis, R Coronae Borealis, U Herculis, R Cygni, U Orionis, S Corona Borealis, Omicron Ceti, Chi Cygni.

PATRICK MOORE: Well-known television personality, author, and expert on astronomy.

General Knowledge 3

121 At the mouth of which river is Dublin situated?

122 Isobars are lines joining places with the same atmospheric pressure. What are isotherms?

123 Women's events made their first appearance in this competition in 1928. Which competition?

124 Stalingrad is now known as Volgograd, what was its original name?

125 What is a line of iambic hexameter called?

126 He became William the Conqueror's Archbishop of Canterbury in 1070. Who was he?

127 The Dutch have a plan to prevent the North Sea inundating the South-western lowlands. What is the plan called?

128 What is an acrostic?

129 From what fruit is the liqueur known as Kirsch distilled?

130 If you had a cadaceus, what would it be?

131 What battle is sometimes called the 'Battle of the Three Emperors'?

132 Most people understand Utopia to mean an impossibly ideal place or state of affairs. What does this word, derived from the Greek, literally mean?

133 His name in particular has become synonymous with political double dealing and intrigue. Who was he?

134 What unique find was made by a Bedouin shepherd boy in a cave in the Wadi Qumran (Qumran Valley)?

135 The lakes of Grasmere, Hawes Water and Rydal Water all lie within which English county?

136 What are the Roman numerals for 400?

137 Who led the 'Huns' of the fourth century AD?

138 Men and women of ancient Greece wore a similar garment. What was it called?

139 In nautical terms, what name is given to the upper edge of a ship's side?

140 Convallaria Majalis is the national flower of Sweden. What is its more common name?

Classical Mythology

Set by Dr Wolfgang Liebeschuetz

141 What was Paris, prince of Troy, doing when the three goddesses, Hera, Aphrodite, and Athena asked him to judge which of them was the fairest?

142 For how long was Troy besieged by the Greeks?

143 How did Achilles die?

144 Why did Orpheus fail to bring back Eurydice from the underworld?

145 What are the names of the couple who survived to re-people the world in the Greek version of the flood legend?

146 Which Greek heroine took poison so that her husband might live?

147 Why did Heracles agree to hold up the heavens?

148 Which reek heroine was hatched from an egg?

149 Which Greek queen played the role of 'Potiphar's wife' to her step-son?

150 Parts of what animals made up the Chimaera?

151 How does Greek religion suggest a connection between commerce and thieving?

152 The Greeks explained the annual return of spring by the story of a rape. Who was the victim?

153 For what offence was Prometheus chained to the Caucasus?

154 What was Oedipus' (correct) answer to the riddle of the Sphinx?

155 Why did the women of Lemnos live without men when the Argonauts arrived?

156 Which level of stratification on the excavated site of Hissarlik is now thought to represent the Troy destroyed by Agamemnon's army?

157 Name the Victorian rediscoverer of the site of Troy.

158 What was the duty of Triptolemus?

159 'A little learning is a dangerous thing, drink deep, or taste not the Pierian spring' (Pope). What was the Pierian spring?

160 The straits leading from the sea of Marmora into the Black Sea are known as the Bosporus. What does the name mean and/or why was it given?

DR WOLFGANG LIEBESCHUETZ: of the Department of Classics, Leicester University.

History of Music 1550-1900

Set by Boswell Taylor

161   By what name is Handel's aria 'Ombra mai fù', composed for his opera *Xerxes*, better known?

162   What is 'opera bouffe'?

163   What is 'The Forty-Eight'?

164   What was the opera that was written for a Chelsea girls' school run by the dancing master, Josias Priest?

165   What form did Mozart's 'Haffner Symphony' take before it became the work we know today?

166   What was the sprightly music often paired with the pavane in the sixteenth century?

167   What is the nickname of Chopin's piano sonata in B flat minor?

168   Who was the Master of the King's Band who composed 'Heart of Oak' to commemorate the British victories in 1759?

169   What is the title of the tunes you play with two fingers on the piano, of which variations have been composed by Borodin, Rimsky-Korsakov and Liszt?

170   What is the title of the operetta that Sullivan composed without Gilbert to a libretto by F. C. Burnand?

171   Who is the heroine of Beethoven's opera *Fidelio*?

172   Many plantation songs, including *The Old Folks at Home* and *Camptown Races*, were composed by whom?

173 What is the generic title of the thirty-six pieces Mendelssohn composed for the piano, among which are three Venetian songs?

174 Why is Schubert's Quintet in A major known as the 'Trout Quintet'?

175 Where did Weber, against considerable opposition, establish a theatre devoted to the performance of opera in German?

176 What music did Beethoven dedicate to the Russian Ambassador in Vienna in 1806?

177 In which city was the first public performance of Handel's *Messiah*?

178 What is the name, meaning 'a pie', which is given to an operatic work such as *Love in a Village*?

179 What island is the setting for Bizet's *The Pearl-Fishers*?

180 Who wrote the drama of French rural life *L'Arlésienne*, for which Bizet composed the incidental music?

General Knowledge 4

181 What is the name of the Greek God of the winds?

182 Victoria Woodhull was the first woman candidate for what office?

183 What is the subtle difference between assault and battery?

184 If you were in a Hummum what would you be most likely to be doing?

185 Born in Stockholm, she first won international fame in a Swedish film *Gosta Berling* in 1924. Who was she?

186 What did William Miller prophesy would happen in 1843?

187 'If all knew what others say about them there would not be four friends in the world' was written by whom?

188 The Norwich School of Painting was founded by whom?

189 Arthur Fitzgibbon was awarded the Victoria Cross in 1861. What was unique about the award?

190 Moscow's church of St Basil the Blessed owes its existence to whom?

191 What is the connection between the Farne Islands and eiderdowns?

192 Who founded the Ballet Russe?

193 Juan Sebastian del Cano commanded a ship called the *Victoria*. What did he achieve in her?

194 Which is the longest river in France?

195 What is the largest known fish in the sea?

196 What name is given to the art and practice of bell ringing?

197 In history, who was 'Hotspur'?

198 The first Dimbleby Lecture was given on BBC television on 31 October 1972. Who delivered it?

199 What is now understood by the phrase 'crossing the Rubicon'?

200 Whose plays fall into two categories, 'pièces noires' and 'pièces roses'?

British Politics Since 1900
Set by Dr David Butler

201 What election in this country yielded the biggest majority?

202 When and why did the Duke of Devonshire resign from the Cabinet?

203 What was 'Mr Balfour's poodle'?

204 How many Parliaments in this country lasted less than a year?

205 Who was Prime Minister for the longest continuous period in this century?

206 What office did Winston Churchill hold for the longest continuous period?

207 When did nationalisation of steel first come into force?

208 When did the Leader of the Opposition first get an official salary?

209 Who brought about a 'bonfire of controls'?

210 Who agreed that who was 'the best Prime Minister we have'?

211 Who said of whom that they were aiming for 'power without responsibility—the prerogative of the harlot throughout the ages'?

212 When did Clement Attlee become Leader of the Labour Party?

213 Who was the first Minister of Technology?

214 When were Life Peers first created?

215 Who introduced Premium Bonds?

216 Why did Sir Samuel Hoare resign from the Cabinet?

217 Who was the first man to resign his peerage?

218 What was the basis for the phrase 'Selsdon Man'?

219 What was the biggest single change in the parity of the pound in this century?

220 What was the Fulton Report?

Dr DAVID E. BUTLER, M.A., D.Phil.: Fellow of Nuffield College, Oxford. Author of: *The British General Election of 1951, The Electoral System in Britain, 1918–1951, The British General Election of 1955, British Political Facts, 1900–1969* etc.

English Costume

Set by Margaret and Boswell Taylor

221 What city is associated with the bright green cloth traditionally worn by Robin Hood?

222 What were 'pomanders'?

223 Who is usually given the credit for inventing 'bloomers'?

224 According to Dickens, Mrs Peerybingle wore 'pattens'. What were these pattens and why were they worn?

225 Still with Dickens, what is a 'Dolly Varden'?

226 Sartorially, what is the difference between a 'Blücher' and a 'Wellington'?

227 Chopin played it. Women wore it. What was the polonaise that women wore in the eighteenth century?

228 The 'liripipe' was not a musical instrument. What was it?

229 In the sixteenth century, how would you have used a 'mocket'?

230 What is a 'billycock'?

231 In the 'naughty nineties', what was a 'gibus'?

232 Sir Walter Scott wrote 'The huntsmen twitched their mauds'. What were their mauds?

233 In the Tudor period a young man might have the choice between wearing 'Spanish slops' or 'Venetians'. What kind of garment were these?

234 In some of the portraits we have of him,
     Shakespeare wore a 'whisk'. What was this?

235 What was known as 'incardine satin'?

236 What was the alternative name that was better
     suited to the bakery than the hatters for the 'high
     Burgundian hat' worn in the fifteenth century?

237 What did a sprig of palm in a traveller's hat in
     Chaucer's time signify?

238 From what article of wear do we get the word
     'sabotage'?

239 In the Dark Ages a peasant might wear a felt hat
     of any colour except yellow. What was the special
     category of person who was obliged to wear a
     yellow hat?

240 To a Victorian, what article of clothing was a
     'bertha'?

Words

Set by Gillian Skirrow and Bill Wright

251 What is the derivation of 'aftermath'?

252 What is neologism?

253 What is the derivation of 'assassin'?

254 What does the word 'maundy' mean?

255 What do the words Bar Mitzvah mean?

256 What is the derivation of the word 'ballot'?

257 The small Australian bear is known as a 'koala'.
    What does 'koala' mean?

258 What is the derivation of the word 'candidate'?

259 What is the derivation of the word 'salary'?

260 What is the derivation of the word 'sandwich'?

General Knowledge 5

261 Lake Erie and Lake Ontario are linked by which canal?

262 'Bailiwick' is a feudal term denoting the limits of a bailiff's jurisdiction. Where is the term still in use today?

263 The American Civil War of 1861 was in the main precipitated by what event?

264 Yabusame is a Japanese version of which sport?

265 Who invented the diesel engine?

266 Which breed of dog is considered to be the tallest?

267 Who was the first of the Lancastrian Kings?

268 The word 'Weald' is the Old English for – what?

269 University College, Cambridge, is to change its name to what?

270 To whom was Churchill referring when he said 'There he stalks, that Wuthering Height'?

271 He lost his head after arranging a marriage between Henry VIII and Anne of Cleves. Who was he?

272 *The Book of Common Prayer* was introduced in 1549 by whom?

273 Who was the author of the collection of short stories entitled *Mortal Coils*?

274 Which character in Shakespeare's *Richard II* described England as 'This precious stone set in the silver sea'?

275 When was the term 'Concentration Camp' first used?

276 What is the name of the Danish Prime Minister who resigned after his country's referendum on the Common Market?

277 He was born Jean Chauvin in Picardy in 1509. By what name is he remembered?

278 What is the English word for the Italian 'Zingaro'?

279 The hero of a Babylonian epic offended the goddess Ishtar and was punished. How was he punished?

280 Baron Passfield helped to found the London School of Economics. By what other name was he known?

British Moths

Set by L. Hugh Newman

281 Which is the most common migrant moth in this country?

282 Which British moth has false eyes in the juvenile stage and turns pink as an adult?

283 Why has the Privet hawk moth been given the generic name of Sphinx?

284 Why is the Peppered moth of special scientific interest?

285 Which British moths contain cyanide?

286 Which British moth has the same colour scheme in the caterpillar stage and as an adult moth?

287 Where was the Waved Black moth first discovered?

288 Which large moth caterpillar has a strong and unpleasant smell?

289 What group of British moths is named after a breed of dog?

290 Which British moth is a silk-spinner, and is related to the tropical silk moths?

291 What British moth was thought to be extinct for nearly a century and was then re-discovered in the East Anglian marshes?

292 Which moth is named after polished metal?

293 What is the deficiency that is common to the Female Winter Moth, the Mottled Umber and the Vapourer?

294 In what way is it true that the Death's Head moth has a voice?

295 What is the common feeding habit of the caterpillars of Clearwing moths?

296 What is the group of British moths named after an almost extinct type of domestic servant?

297 How is it possible for male moths to locate females in the dark?

298 In the lepidopteral sense, why is the small Puss moth caterpillar not a kitten?

299 What kind of weather do moths prefer for their noctural jaunts?

300 In what way is the male Ghost moth ghostlike?

L. HUGH NEWMAN, F.R.E.S.: Managing Director, Butterfly Farm. Author of: *Butterfly Farmer* (Phoenix House), *British Moths in their Haunts* (Edmund Ward), etc.

English Literature
Set by Boswell Taylor

301 Who was the fifteenth-century jail-bird who wrote a classic romance of knighthood?

302 Who was the Shakespearian heroine who disguised herself as Ganymede after 'Jove's own page'?

303 What is the title of the important book on education written by Queen Elizabeth the First's childhood tutor?

304 Who was the titled recipient of Dr Samuel Johnson's famous letter upon his patronage?

305 There were two main contributors to the first numbers of *The Tatler* and *The Spectator*. One was Sir Richard Steele, who was the other?

306 What is the literary term introduced into our language by John Lyly?

307 What famous nineteenth-century novelist attempted to clear off a debt of more than £100,000 with a succession of novels?

308 What is the real name of the village of Cranford?

309 Christopher Marlowe and John Donne each begin a poem with the identical first line. What was that line?

310 What is the title of the novel that Henry Fielding wrote as a parody of Richardson's *Pamela?*

311 What is the book in which Charles Dickens attacked the lust for money through inheritance and the Chancery Court?

312 What is the reasoning in the choice of 'Erewhon' as the title of Samuel Butler's satire?

313 Of what school were Stalky and Co. pupils?

314 Who was the author of *Curiosa Mathematica* and *Notes on the First Two Books of Euclid*?

315 Wycherley and Congreve were two of the main writers of comedies of manners, who was the third?

316 Who did Thomas Thorpe, the publisher, claim to be 'the onlie begetter of these insuing sonnets'?

317 What was the political position ultimately achieved by the author of *Coningsby*?

318 What famous work had its genesis in a back room of Tom Davies's bookshop at No. 8 Russell Street, Covent Garden?

319 Who is Edgar Allan Poe's detective, said to have been the first of a prolific line of fictional detectives?

320 What were the actual names of the authors who wrote as Currer, Ellis and Acton Bell?

Tudor History
Set by John D. Bareham

321 Who was the royal officer sent by Henry VII to govern Ireland for him (his name was given to the laws which settled the relationship between the English and Irish Parliaments of the time)?

322 Which famous Netherlands' writer and philosopher came to lecture in Oxford in 1498?

323 One of the so-called Commonwealth Men, John Hales, was the moving spirit behind a commission in 1548 which investigated an important social and economic problem. What was this problem?

324 Who led a rebellion against Queen Mary Tudor in 1554, partly against the Spanish marriage?

325 What connection is there between Bishops Hooper, Ridley and Latimer, apart from their being Protestants in doctrine?

326 What happened on Evil May Day 1517 in London?

327 Who wrote 'The Assertion of the Seven Sacraments', in 1521, a defence of the Church against Luther?

328 How was English life affected in 1563 by an attempt to encourage seamen and seamanship?

329 When and what was the 'Whip with Six Strings'?

330 Princess Mary Tudor married Louis XII of France. Who was her second husband?

331 With what art or craft do you associate Wynkyn de Worde?

332 Local historians and demographers have reason to be pleased with Thomas Cromwell's instructions to the English parish clergy of 1538. Why?

333 Whose life was Queen Elizabeth I forced to sacrifice to the executioner, in order to save Mary Queen of Scots' life when it was threatened by Parliament and the Council?

334 The traditional Parliamentary tax of the Tudors was the Fifteenth and the Tenth. What was this?

335 Who came back to England in 1548, on leave of absence from Spain, and spent the last ten years of his life teaching the English the art of navigation?

336 What was Sir Christopher Hatton's cognizance, from his coat of arms (remembered most because of his investment in sea voyages)?

337 Professor Hoskins maintains that standard historians of the Tudor period neglect one vital factor causing sixteenth-century discontent. He mentions particularly troubles in 1549–51, during Edward VI's reign. What factor does he stress?

338 A famous Elizabethan miniature painter born about 1547 was the first English-born artist to leave details of his own life and work. Who was he?

339 Professor Scarisbrick has urged a particular theory regarding Cardinal Wolsey's foreign policy. Which is his main theme: (a) Wolsey the servant of Henry VIII; (b) Wolsey hoping to become Pope; (c) Wolsey the Peace-maker?

340 One of the great problems of historians of the Tudor period is to estimate the population of England; no figure is more than an estimate, but there has been much modern research. According to Professor J. C. Russell and Mr Julian Cornwall, about what figure was the population of England at about the end of the reign of Henry VIII (1545–7)?

JOHN D. BAREHAM: Senior History Lecturer, Exeter College.

General Knowledge 6

341 A member of the family *Alaudidae*, Wordsworth wrote a poem in his praise. Who is he?

342 Which author did Hitler and Mussolini acclaim as the master prophet of right-wing authoritarianism?

343 Indonesia was declared a Republic in 1945. Who was its First President?

344 The French gendarme wears a distinctive hat. What is it called?

345 At sea what period of time is covered by the first 'Dog Watch'?

346 They were founded in the reign of Henry VII for the protection of the Royal Person. Who were they?

347 Her first major success was in the film *The Blue Angel*. Who was she?

348 It was designed by Robert Fulton and tried out in the Seine in 1801. What was it?

349 He wrote many of the plays known as 'The Aldwych Farces' in the 1920s such as *Rookery Nook*. Who was he?

350 For what would you use a Wheatstone Bridge?

351 His first novel was *Desperate Remedies* and his last was *Jude the Obscure*. Who was he?

352 What fortunate discovery was made by Jacobus Jonker in 1934?

353 Where did the game squash originate?

354 What do the letters P.V.C. stand for?

355 Among his famous musicals were *The Vagabond King* and *Rose Marie*. Who was he?

356 In sailing, what is a 'jury mast'?

357 Who used the pseudonyms Diedrich Knickerbocker and Jonathan Oldstyle among others?

358 T. S. Eliot wrote, 'He always has an alibi, and one or two to spare; At whatever time the deed took place – Macavity wasn't there'. Who was Macavity?

359 First Baron Tweedsmuir, he was at one time the Governor-General of Canada, and wrote many successful adventure stories. Who was he?

360 In 1877 he constructed the phonograph, which he called 'the Ideal Amanuensis'. Who was he?

Assassinations and Murders

Set by Boswell Taylor

361 How many presidents of the United States have been assassinated?

362 Who is the only British Prime Minister to be assassinated?

363 Where was he assassinated?

364 What was the play that Abraham Lincoln saw the night that he was assassinated?

365 Who is alleged to have been assassinated by Nazi agents on 25 July 1934?

366 Who assassinated the Duke of Buckingham in 1628?

367 In which city did the assassination of Martin Luther King take place?

368 Lee Oswald was accused of shooting John Kennedy, the President of the United States. Who shot Lee Oswald?

369 Who was the king of Yugoslavia who was assassinated in Marseille in 1934?

370 When Archduke Francis Ferdinand was assassinated in 1914, his wife died with him, what was her name?

371 Who assassinated Robert Kennedy?

372 Who was assassinated by a Hindu fanatic as he was on his way to a prayer meeting on 30 January 1948?

373 In the Maybrick case, according to the prosecution what was the source of the poison used by Florence Maybrick to murder her husband?

374 Where was Ronald True when he was arrested for the murder of Gertrude Yates?

375 Whose love letters are said to have led to the murder of her husband and her execution in the nineteen-twenties?

376 Who was the infamous dweller in the notorious No. 10 Rillington Place, North Kensington?

377 Who was the last woman in Britain to be hanged?

378 What was the verdict in the Madeleine Smith trial in the 1850s?

379 What was the unusual defence put forward for Guenther Fritz Podola when he was tried for the murder of Detective Sergeant Purdy?

380 Who was the well-known pathologist who was concerned in both the Seddon case and the Edith Thompson trial?

Visual Arts

Set by Richard Francis

381 Picasso's *Guernica* was a protest about the bombing by Spanish planes of a village. What was the year when the event took place that inspired the painting?

382 Name the artist who was responsible for the windows in the new cathedral at Coventry.

383 Whose political monument which won Grand Prize in an international competition in 1953 caused an aggressive public response?

384 A famous architect died whilst swimming in 1965. He was responsible for the design of *La Tourette* amongst many other famous buildings. Who was he?

385 With which printmaker do you associate *Atelier 17* and new ways of gravure?

386 What is an icon?

387 Over the south door of Sancta Sophia, Constantine presents a model of the city and Justinian one of the church to a figure on the throne. Whom does the figure represent?

388 Completed around 1190, where is a mosaic cycle showing Christ's miracles?

389 A leader of the avant-garde in the 1920s, late in life he took to drawing from earlier masters. A museum is dedicated to his work in Biot. Who was he?

390 *Creation and Crucifixion* won the first prize at the first John Moore's Exhibition at Liverpool. Who was the prizewinner?

391 What was Anthony Caro's connection with the *New Generation*?

392 Who was the first American painter to win the *Venice Biennale*?

393 What is the name of the Byzantine cathedral of Constantinople?

394 Two major exhibitions in 1971 were closed soon after the opening. The first, in New York, was of photographs by Hans Haache; the second, in London, was by another American artist, who was he?

395 Who is the Professor of Sculpture at the Kunstakademie in Düsseldorf?

396 Where would you find the eleventh-century apse mosaic *The Virgin with Apostles*?

397 Which painter since the war do you associate with the iconic image of a flag?

398 What is the subject of the squinch in the dome of the church of Daphni near Athens, where Christ dominates the open space in the vaults?

399 At what date did Iconoclasm end?

400 What is the 'Joshua Roll'?

History of Aeronautics

Set by Charles Gibbs-Smith

401 Who made the first cross-channel flight in an aeroplane?

402 One of the two earliest airborne aeronautical devices was the kite. What was the other?

403 Venice was the first city to be bombed from the air. How was it done?

404 Who first crossed the Channel by air?

405 What was the first machine to attempt to cross the English Channel?

406 What world-famous light aeroplane first flew in 1925?

407 What was the first turbo-jet aeroplane to fly?

408 By what aerodynamic means did the Germans intend to increase the range of their A-4 rocket bomb, popularly called the V-2?

409 In 1931 the RAF won the Schneider Trophy outright. With what machine did they achieve this?

410 The first fatal accident in a powered aeroplane was in 1908. Name one of the two passengers in the plane.

411 What single make of aero-engine was the mainstay of early European aviation?

412 The first aerial passenger service runs were made between 1910 and 1914. Where?

413 By whom was the first parachute jump made from the air?

414   What was the accepted technique of survival in Victorian ballooning?

415   Who flew the first circle in an aeroplane?

416   Why did not the aeronautical drawings and writings of Leonardo da Vinci play any part in inspiring any pioneer in the history of the aeroplane?

417   What was peculiar about the functioning of the tailplane on Otto Lilienthal's standard and later gliders?

418   How was control-in-roll effected in Louis Blériot's successful cross-Channel monoplane?

419   What directly inspired the familiar early configuration of biplane wings and forward elevators?

420   Who was the first man to fit ailerons or elevons to a full-size aircraft?

CHARLES H. GIBBS-SMITH, M.A., F.M.A., F.R.S.A., Chevalier Danish Order of the Dannebrog, Keeper Emeritus, Victoria and Albert Museum. Author: *A History of Flying* (Batsford), *The Aeroplane, An Historical Survey* (H.M.S.O.) etc.

General Knowledge 7

421 In mythology, what were Medusa, Stheno and Euryale collectively known as?

422 Who assassinated Jean Paul Marat?

423 In which country is the temple of Amun at Karnak?

424 Which English composer was a pupil of John Blow and became organist of Westminster Abbey in 1679?

425 What is the basic law of magnetism?

426 What is the meaning of symbiosis?

427 Where would you find a martingale?

428 In which English county do these rivers flow: Teme, Frome, Lugg, Dore, Arrow and Monnow?

429 Joseph Smith founded a religious sect in 1830. What is it called?

430 He edited the 'North Briton', was outlawed, and later became Lord Mayor of London. Who was he?

431 Who founded Oxford University's Christ Church College?

432 What are the Hagiographs?

433 What family ruled Austria from the thirteenth century to 1918?

434 Who describes his journeys as a young man from his Gloucestershire village to London, and finally Spain and the Civil War?

435 Who followed Friedrich Ebert as President of the Weimar Republic?

436 Stoke, Burslem, Longton, Hanley and Tunstall are collectively known as what?

437 What name is given to the painting medium that uses the yolks of eggs?

438 Boadicea or Boudicca, queen of the Iceni, died in the time of which Roman emperor?

439 Von Reuter ordered the scuttling of the German Fleet in 1919. Where was it scuttled?

440 He was a musician, the son of a poor school teacher, born in Vienna in 1797, and he died there in 1828. Who was he?

Old Time Music Hall

Set by Peter Davison

441 In what year did George Formby senior die?

442 What was Sam Collin's original profession?

443 Who sang, 'If you want to know the time, ask a P'liceman'?

444 In what year did the Metropolitan finally close?

445 Who was 'The woman who knows'?

446 When did the music hall strike begin?

447 Who tried to close the Empire Promenade in the 1890s?

448 When the Promenade was partitioned off, what man, later a Prime Minister, helped break it down?

449 What performer was shot by his father in a fit of jealousy?

450 Who was 'The Essence of Eccentricity'?

451 What was the name of the music-hall performer who was murdered by her husband in 1910?

452 Who was the mesmerist with whom, in effect, George Robey began his professional career?

453 Who first sang 'It's a long way to Tipperary'?

454 Who was 'John Bull's Girl'?

455 Who, before becoming a university professor, wrote for Marie Lloyd?

456 Who sang a song called 'The Lambeth Walk' at the end of the nineteenth century?

457 Which music hall was called 'The Royal Academy over the Water'?

458 Who, in 1878, sang in a song 'I ain't a Briton true'?

459 What was the music hall at which George Ridley sang 'Blaydon Races'?

460 What were the subjects of the three songs Dan Leno sang to Edward VII?

Chemistry

Set by R. A. Ross

461 For what is the chemist Newlands remembered?

462 Mendeleev, on the basis of his Periodic Table, predicted the properties of some, at the time, unknown elements. One he called eka-silicon. What was it called when it was discovered?

463 What is the name of the element whose symbol is Pm?

464 Prometheum belongs to a group of elements. What is the group called?

465 The group of fourteen elements called Lanthanides have very similar chemical properties. How is the similarity explained?

466 Relative atomic masses are defined in terms of carbon 12. Why does the carbon in graphite have a relative atomic mass of 12.011?

467 Can you, in theory, have a mole of mice?

468 Approximately, how many mice in a mole of mice?

469 What is the thermicity of the reaction between carbon and oxygen?

470 What is the sign of the enthalpy change for such a reaction?

471 Which is the odd man out of the following list and why: sodium, potassium, barium and cesium?

472 What have haemoglobin, copper tetramine sulphate and potassium ferriferrocyanide in common?

473 What is the crystal structure of sodium chloride?

474 How was sodium first prepared, and by whom?

475 In representing organic compounds we use a line to stand for a bond. This represents two electrons shared. This method does not work for benzene. What is the phenomenon responsible for this failure called?

476 How many different compounds have the formula C H Cl Br F?

477 How are these substances distinguishable?

478 Why does hexene decolorise a solution of bromine?

479 What is the hydrogen ion concentration in pure water?

480 Why is 0.1 mole per litre acetic acid called a weak acid?

History of the English Language

Set by A. A. Evans and Boswell Taylor

481 The prefix 'geo' is derived from the Greek. What was its original meaning?

482 In the consonant shift *k* became *h;* what did *p* become?

483 In the history of the English language what period is covered by 'Old English'?

484 There are several river Avons in England. What did the name 'Avon' mean originally?

485 What is a mutated plural?

486 Why are the uplands of southern England called Downs?

487 What is the special name sometimes applied to Scottish and Irish Gaelic?

488 Madrigals are associated with Elizabethan England, but from which language did the English borrow the word?

489 We took the word 'tea' from the Chinese. From which language did we get 'coffee'?

490 How did the word 'boycott', meaning to have nothing to do with a person, get into the English language?

491 What is the derivation of the word whisky?

492 What were the meanings of the two Greek words that scientists used to make the word *chlorophyll?*

493 What are the elements that make up the word *ampersand?*

494   Who was the Scottish novelist who helped to popularise the use of Scottish words in the early part of the nineteenth century?

495   What name is often given to the series of changes in the long vowels which took place in late Middle English and Early Modern English?

496   What is the derivation of the town-crier's repeated 'Oyez'?

497   Old English script used seven vowel symbols: *a e i o u* and *y* and another one. What was the seventh vowel symbol?

498   Why did Francis Bacon, who had published his *Advancement in Learning* in 1605 in English, have it re-published in Latin later?

499   Why the 'by' in By-law?

500   What would be the most likely pronounciation that a member of the Victorian upper-classes would give to the word we know as cucumber?

General Knowledge 8

501 Where was Hitler's mountain hideout?

502 Who was the admiral and hydrographer who gave his name to a 'scale' that described the force of winds?

503 In 1519 the *Trinidad*, *San Antonio*, *Concepcion*, *Victoria*, and *Santiago* made up the fleet of a famous explorer. Who was he?

504 Among the plays he has written are *Photo Finish* and *Romanoff and Juliet*. Who is he?

505 They are ancient Hindu scriptures, written in an old form of Sanskrit. What are they called?

506 What is the mark called that fixes the maximum load line of a merchant vessel in salt water?

507 What is the longest river in Scotland?

508 In Britain the sovereign has three crowns, what are they?

509 Newton was at one time its President and it first received the Royal Charter in 1662. What was it?

510 Which English king was born at Caernarvon Castle in 1284 and ended his life in Berkeley Castle?

511 Can you name two of the pictures illustrated musically by Mussorgsky in his composition *Pictures at an Exhibition*?

512 The Lord Chamberlain's men were a theatrical company. Who was their most famous member?

513 His first play *Catalina* was published in 1850. Who was he?

514 By what name is the painter Domenicos Theotocopoulos, who lived from 1541-1614, better known?

515 Alexei Leonov marked up a first in space exploration. What did he achieve?

516 Who, in Greek mythology, were Clotho, Lachesis and Atropos?

517 His Latin name was Carolus Magnus. Who was he?

518 Vintners mark them on each side, but those belonging to the Crown are unmarked. What are they?

519 In 1572 who observed a nova in the constellation of Cassiopeia?

520 Cardinal John Newman was the author of *The Dream of Gerontius*. Who set it to music?

Sea and Ships
Set by Alan Villiers

521 How many ropes are there in a full-rigged ship?

522 Teodor Nalecz Korzeniowski is associated with the sea. In what way?

523 What was the name by which Drake's famous ship was known before his circumnavigation?

524 Who was the 'doctor' at sea in sailing-ship days?

525 What speed records are held by the clipper-ship *Cutty Sark*?

526 Which was the first true steamship to cross the Atlantic?

527 How long has the Suez Canal been closed?

528 What is the name of the first nuclear-powered sea-going vessel?

529 What is the deepest known spot in the world's oceans?

530 What percentage of the earth's surface is covered by the oceans (approx.)?

531 What was the special feature of the British ship *Vulcan* built in 1818?

532 Name the first nuclear-powered merchant ship.

533 What was the name of the first propeller-driven ship to cross the Atlantic?

534 What did Cook's ship have in common with Colonel Scott's Apollo 15 space shot recently?

535 What are the following vessels noted for: *SS Waratah;* the four-masted barque, *Admiral Karpfanger;* the Brazilian battleship *Sao Paulo*?

536 Aboard ship, what is (or was) meant by the term 'Tell-tale'?

537 What was a bald-headed square-rigged ship?

538 How would you set about putting a model ship in a bottle?

539 Why was the non-commissioned officer James Cook selected to command the British *Endeavour* expedition in 1768?

540 Which well-known discoverer turned back from the Coral Sea when on the point of preceding Captain Cook to the discovery of Australia's East Coast?

ALAN J. VILLIERS: Trustee, National Maritime Museum, President of the Society for Nautical Research, Governor Cutty Sark Society. Author: *Cruise of the 'Conrad', Quest of the Schooner 'Argus'* etc.

Medical Science
Set by Professor A. J. Harding Rains

541 What does the abbreviation E.C.G. stand for?

542 How large is the blood volume in an average adult male?

543 What is haemorrhage which takes place 7-14 days after operation or injury called?

544 What is the volume of air normally inspired and expired at each breath called?

545 What is gastrin?

546 What group of organisms may cause gas gangrene and tetanus?

547 Name the skin test for susceptibility or immunity to diptheria.

548 What is scotopic vision?

549 What are the large molecular complexes which form bile acids?

550 What is the second-set phenomenon?

551 What chemical substance is released from the blood platelets?

552 What is the anti-bacterial advantage in sucking a cut finger?

553 Which vitamin may be found in sewage and sludge?

554 When can you hear the sounds of Korotkow?

555 What are Betz cells?

556 What is a Rad?

557 What is an anamnestic reaction?

558 What is an absolute refractory period?

559 What is After-discharge?

560 What are the powerful shock-producing
polypeptides liberated in the plasma (fortunately
destroyed rapidly)?

PROFESSOR A. J. HARDING RAINS, M.S., F.R.C.S.,
Professor of Surgery, Charing Cross Hospital Medical
School.

Antiques

Set by Arthur Negus

561 What was the principal wood used by Thomas Chippendale during the eighteenth century?

562 What is the main difference between pottery and porcelain?

563 Glass paperweights were produced in France, circa 1848 at Baccarat, Clichy and one other factory. Name the factory.

564 What is the present sterling standard of silver required by British Law?

565 Thomas Bolsover invented an efficient substitute for silver about 1745 – what was it called?

566 Shark-skin, often dyed green, was used for covering cases which held scientific instruments. What was this material called?

567 Seventeenth-century needlework with raised padded portions of the design was used on caskets, can you name it?

568 Name the firm that sponsored 'Art Nouveau' in England.

569 What was the original Portland Vase called?

570 Messrs Chippendale, Adam, Hepplewhite and Sheraton gave their names to definite styles of furniture; who are the 'odd ones out' in the four?

571 Early English oak is sometimes inlaid with a white wood – what is it?

572 Only three factories in England make hard-paste porcelain. Newhall in its early days, name the other two.

573 Rosewood is a good hard wood; what other woods from the same genus (Dalbergia) are allied to it?

574 What is fore-edge painting?

575 Can you name the type of clock made of brass during the seventeenth century with hinged side doors, a dome surmount and pierced frets?

576 What is a dummy board figure?

577 Can you name the flower painter who followed William Billingsley at Derby circa 1795?

578 When a picture is painted composed of opaque colours and gum, what term is used to describe it?

579 Describe briefly a *cheveret*.

580 Chests in the sixteenth century were inlaid with conventional representations of buildings – can you give a name to this type?

ARTHUR NEGUS: Well-known television personality and expert on antiques. Author of: *Going for a Song* (BBC).

General Knowledge 9

581 On the hundredth anniversary of American
Independence the people of France made a
presentation to the American people. What was it?

582 During the First World War the British soldier
was known as a 'Tommy': what name was given
to the French soldiers?

583 From 1881 Russian Jews and their property were
subjected to periodic mob attacks. What were
these attacks called?

584 What is the anatomical name for your shoulder
blade?

585 In the fictional submarine *Nautilus* who was the
Captain?

586 Plymouth, Massachusetts, was founded in the
1600s by what group of people?

587 During the troubles in Cyprus, who was the leader
of the movement known as Eoka?

588 Which regiment of the British Army were known
as 'Pontius Pilate's Bodyguard'?

589 Who wrote the play *The Passing of the Third Floor
Back*?

590 Eamon de Valera founded the Irish Fianna Fail
party in 1926. What is the English translation of
'Fianna Fail'?

591 At the Diet of Worms in 1521 what was defended?

592 What are the 'White Horses' of Westbury and
Uffington?

593 Who professed his love in these lines: 'I cry your mercy – pity – love! – aye, love! Merciful love that tantalised not...'?

594 Who wrote *Chips with Everything* and *Roots* among other plays?

595 In 1858 Bernadette Soubrious was witness to a supernatural event. Where did it take place?

596 Her real name was Frances Gumm but under what name did she rise to stardom?

597 Who was the soldier/statesman whose picture appears on the back of the English £5 note?

598 Who proved that all falling objects have the same velocity whether large or small?

599 Who were the Kamikaze of the Second World War?

600 The Biblical Solomon was the son of David; who was his mother?

Gardening

Set by Professor Alan Gemmell

601 What is topiary?

602 What is the name of the pollen-producing part of a flower?

603 What is hydroponics?

604 What is a 'piping' and what is it used for?

605 What is the name of a disease which attacks the cabbage and cauliflower family (brassicas) and causes swellings of the roots?

606 How would you prune a newly planted hybrid tea rose bush?

607 What distance below the surface should you sow carrot seed?

608 In gardening what is ph?

609 What is tilth?

610 When do you prune plums?

611 What was the name of the great British landscape gardener of the eighteenth century?

612 What is the art of bonsai?

613 A white frothy liquid is produced on plants by the frog hopper insect, what is it called?

614 If I were marcotting a shaddock what would I be doing?

615 Only one of the following will tolerate a limy soil. Which is it: (a) Camellia indica (b) Pieris forrestii or (c) Erica cinerea?

616 What is the botanical name for African Violet?

617 What does it mean when a potato is said to be 'immune'?

618 What is the meaning of MM106?

619 If the apical (or terminal) bud of a chrysanthemum is removed a number of side shoots or breaks will arise. What is the name of the apical bud on one of these side shoots?

620 If Pitmaston Duchess has 51 how many has Louise Bonne de Jersey?

PROFESSOR ALAN R. GEMMELL: Professor of Biology at Keele University, well-known radio personality in gardening programmes.

Mammals

Set by Dr L. Harrison Matthews

621 Do any female deer normally have antlers, and if so, which?

622 Name two British mammals that hibernate.

623 When a baby kangaroo is born how does it get into the mother's pouch?

624 One of the possums of Australia and New Guinea is called the 'Ring-Tailed Possum'. Why?

625 Which mammal has a natural sun-burn lotion?

626 Name one mammal, other than man, that uses tools.

627 Camels when excited often protrude from the mouth a thing like a pink toy balloon called the palu. What exactly is it?

628 What mammal is the natural host of the myxoma virus?

629 Name one mammal that has a poisonous bite that paralyses small prey.

630 The honey-guide (Indicator) is an African bird. What mammal does it guide to honey?

631 Which mammal has its liver so packed with vitamin A that the liver kills you if you eat it?

632 The walrus makes a musical sound like striking a church bell. How?

633 Which mammals often anoint themselves with foamy saliva when stimulated by a strange odour?

634 What do sea-cows – manatees and dugongs – eat when in the sea (some live in fresh water)?

635 Which mammal carries what is known as a pearl necklace?

636 Two kinds of bats habitually eat fish. Name one of them.

637 How do these bats catch fish?

638 Of all the kinds of antelope only one has been domesticated. Which one?

639 All the toothed-whales have a more or less rounded forehead filled with oily fat called the 'melon'. What is its function?

640 Mammals have a normal body temperature of about 37°C. Apart from hibernating, which normally has the lowest?

Dr L. HARRISON MATTHEWS: Former Director London Zoo.

641 It was a tenth part of a legion and consisted of 600 infantrymen. What was it called?

642 Between 1763 and 1767 two English surveyors drew a line separating the old slave States of America from the free state of Pennsylvania. Who were they?

643 Drosophila have been of great assistance in the study of genetics. What are they?

644 Where did Edward II die?

645 The tradition of summoning MP's by Black Rod from the House of Commons to the House of Lords dates from which event?

646 Which mountain was sacred to Apollo and the Muses?

647 The zenith is a point on the celestial sphere. What is the point directly opposite to it?

648 Who was the originator of the Penny Post?

649 Which former home for disabled soldiers contains Napoleon's tomb?

650 Which famous man's ancestors lived at Sulgrave Manor, Northamptonshire?

651 Brutus and Cassius were defeated at Philippi by whom?

652 Historically, what was the Heptarchy?

653 Which composer wrote works as *Moments Mikrophonie I and II* and *Mixtur* among others?

654 What is the highest peak in Northern Ireland?

655 What is the better known title for the operetta called *The Peer and the Peri*?

656 How did Lord Kitchener die?

657 Who was the Russian physiologist best known for his experimental work on animal behaviour, particularly conditioned reflexes in animals?

658 In which sport are these terms used: 'bull-pen' and 'strike-out'?

659 Usually every human being has twenty-three pairs of these, what are they?

660 $E = MC^2$ is a formula for which theory?

Scandinavian Mythology

Set by Professor Peter Foote

661 Which Eddiac poem appears to reflect a ritual of 'sacred marriage' with Frey (Freyr) as the male partner?

662 From whom are the gods supposed to have learnt the shamanistic kind of magic called *seid* or *seithur*?

663 What is Aurvandil's toe?

664 Whose hearing was so keen that he could hear wool growing on sheep?

665 What does a Norse poet mean when he refers to 'tears of Freyja' and 'hair of Sif'?

666 Which god had the central place in the temple at Uppsala according to Adam of Bremen?

667 Which Danish island and Swedish lake are said to match because of the ploughing of Gefujn?

668 There are two main groups of divinities of Norse mythology, aesir is one of them, what is the other?

669 What is the name of the chief prose source for Scandinavian mythology?

670 What is *Skidbladnir* (or *Skithblathnir*)?

671 Why does a Norse poet call the sky the 'labour of Austri'?

672 Tacitus describes a female divinity who appears to have the same name as one of the Vanir gods; what are their names?

673 Which exploit of Thor's is sculpted on stones at Altuna in Sweden and Hordum in Denmark?

674 Which is counted the more original expression, Ragnarok 'doom of the gods', or Ragnarokk(u)r 'twilight of the gods'?

675 What, in Norse mythology, is counted the equivalent of Noah's Flood?

676 Noise of a cat, spittle of a bird, beard of a woman, breath of a fish, roots of a rock, sinews of a bear were ingredients to make what?

677 After dwarves killed Kvasir how did they explain his death to the gods?

678 How, according to Adam of Bremen, did the Swedes regard Thor?

679 Where have scholars chiefly detected Christian influence on Norse mythology?

680 There are three main divisions of the system postulated by Dumezil and others for Indo-European religion supposedly represented by Norse gods. Sovereign gods and Warrior gods are two, what is the third?

PROFESSOR PETER FOOTE, Professor of Old Scandinavian and Director of Scandinavian Studies, University College, London, Secretary, Viking Society, Chevalier, Icelandic Order of the Falcon.
Author: *The Viking Achievement* etc.

Scottish History

Set by Nigel Tranter

681 What is the Battle of Otterburn generally called in England?

682 Who used an arm to bar a door against a King's attackers?

683 What is the link between an Oxford College and an old Dumfries bridge?

684 What does a black bull's head served on a platter mean in Scottish history?

685 When did a force of Spaniards last fight on Scottish soil?

686 What was the name of Rob Roy's wife?

687 What two Scots brothers were monarchs at the same time?

688 Who was captured in a hollow tree on an island?

689 What was the name of the ship which finally bore Prince Charlie from Scotland to France?

690 What part did the Dewars play in old Scotland?

691 What were the Spanish Blanks?

692 What clause, offered by the English in the Treaty of Northampton, was surprisingly ignored by the Scots?

693 What bloody deed was heralded by reports of a stranger with a black cloak and a pot of gold?

694 What was the Trot of Turriff?

695 What was the Brooch of Lorn?

696 Donald, Lord of the Isles, led one side at the Battle of Harlaw in 1411 – who led the other?

697 Who worded the famous Declaration of Independence, 1320?

698 Where did King Charles the Second sign the Solemn League and Covenant?

699 What was the game known as Hurly Hackit?

700 Who were the Joint Guardians who succeeded William Wallace as Guardian of Scotland in 1298?

NIGEL TRANTER: Author of many novels set in Scotland and about Scottish heroes, one of the most recent being *Robert the Bruce*. Now compiling a ten-volume series *The Queen's Scotland*.

First World War

Set by Bill Wright

701 In what year was poison gas used for the first time?

702 The Germans called it the Siegfried Line, what did the Allies call it?

703 Why are the 'Old Contemptibles' so called?

704 What historical event took place on 28 July 1914?

705 A strategic base for the German fleet in World War 1 once belonged to Britain for over a hundred years. What was it?

706 Where did General Ludendorff and General Hindenburg crush the Russian armies in 1914?

707 In 1917 which King was forced by an ultimatum from the Allies to abdicate in favour of his son?

708 What were Tabloids, Pups and Camels?

709 Which British towns were attacked by the first Zeppelin raid of the war?

710 Which forces were engaged at the Battle of Lemberg?

711 On what plan did Germany base its war strategy?

712 Who was the Turkish War Minister who virtually took command of the troops in the field during the Dardanelles campaign?

713 In 1916 peace proposals were addressed to America and other nations. Who initiated these proposals?

714 The allies established an army at Salonika in October 1915. What was the object of this?

715 Where did a British fleet destroy Vice-Admiral Maximilian Von Spee's fleet?

716 With what theatre of war would you associate these place names; Achi Baba, Sari Bair and Kilid Bahr?

717 Which troops stormed Vimy Ridge in 1917?

718 At which battle were tanks used on a large scale?

719 Whom did the Allies appoint Generalissimo over the Western Front in 1918?

720 The Japanese delivered an ultimatum to Germany on 23 August 1914 demanding that Germany relinquish the leased territory she possessed. Where was this?

721 What kind of character was 'Gargantua' created by Rabelais?

722 James Loveless, George Loveless, James Hammett, James Brine, Thomas Standfield and John Standfield became known as what?

723 What gets burnt at 'Up-Helly-A'?

724 What did John Stutter start in 1848?

725 What was the name of the standard mathematics book used for over 2,000 years?

726 His pen name was 'Saki'. What was his real name?

727 Henry VI of France gave full freedom of worship to the Protestants in 1598. What was this decree called?

728 Percy Shaw's invention has been a boon to motorists. What was it?

729 Who invented the conspiracy known as the Popish Plot?

730 What in the scientific world is known as Zeta?

731 According to Greek mythology who was the first woman on earth?

732 In musical terms, who was the 'Bringer of Jollity'?

733 What was the function of the Press Gangs of the early nineteenth century?

734 What access did the Polish corridor provide for Poland after the First World War?

735 A famous allegory was written in Bedford gaol. What was the title?

736 Which Queen of England married her brother-in-law?

737 The French call it 'La Tapisseri de la Reine Matilde'. What do we call it?

738 In Roman times gladiators were matched against opponents carrying tridents and nets. What name was given to a trident carrier?

739 Gertrude Ederle of USA achieved a famous first. What was her achievement?

740 Who virtually ruled Florence between 1469 and 1492?

Poetry

Set by Boswell Taylor

741   If a stately Spanish galleon 'had a cargo of diamonds, emeralds, amethysts, topazes and cinnamon and gold moidores', what kind of ship carried 'Tyne coal, road-rails, pig-lead, firewood, iron-ware and cheap tin trays'?

742   What was the famous anthology that first included William Wordsworth's 'Lines written above Tintern Abbey'?

743   Who was the girl that Robert Burns wished to toast in 'a pint o' wine, An' fill it in a silver tassie . . .'?

744   What was the nickname by which James Hogg was generally known?

745   Of which bird does Wordsworth ask 'shall I call thee bird, Or but a wandering Voice'?

746   Who is the modern poet who declared: 'Time held me green and dying, Though I sang in my chains like the sea . . .'?

747   What was the relationship between Sohrab and Rustum in Matthew Arnold's famous poem?

748   What is the pen-name of Christopher Murray Grieve?

749   What was the creature that D. H. Lawrence mourned because 'Her bright striped frost-face will never watch any more, out of the shadow of the cave in the blood-orange rock'?

750   Which of Chaucer's pilgrims asked to be: 'excused of my rude speche. I lerned nevere rethorik, certayn; Thyng that I speke, it moot be bare and pleyn. I sleep nevere on the Mount of Pernaso, Ne lerned Marcu Tullius Scithero . . .'?

751 What is the title of the poem Edmund Spenser wrote to celebrate his marriage in 1594?

752 What is R. L. Stevenson's own epitaph which is inscribed on his gravestone?

753 Which section is missing from this list of T. S. Eliot's *Four Quartets: The Dry Savages, Burnt Norton, Little Gidding*?

754 Which of Sir Walter Scott's poems is sub-titled 'A Tale of Flodden Field, in Six Cantos'?

755 What is the first line of Wordsworth's sonnet 'Upon Westminster Bridge'?

756 In the poem that begins 'Why should I find Him here And not in a Church', where does Jack Clemo find Christ?

757 What was the name of Oliver Goldsmith's 'Deserted Village'?

758 According to John Milton in an early sonnet what, 'hath time, the subtle thief of youth, stolen on his wing . . .'?

759 What was the happening that made Keats look: 'like stout Cortez when with eagle eyes, he stared at the Pacific'?

760 What modern poet turned a sergeant's instructions on the naming of parts of a rifle into a poem he called 'Lessons of the War – Naming of Parts'?

Astronomy 2
Set by Patrick Moore

761 What is believed to be the main constituent of the Martian atmosphere?

762 What distinguished position has been held by James Bradley, Nevil Maskelyne, and Edmund Halley among others?

763 What spectacular event happened in Siberia in 1908?

764 Name a famous philosopher of classical Greece who maintained that the Earth goes round the Sun, not vice versa.

765 During the last century a planet was said to exist close to the Sun, with its orbit within that of Mercury. What was it called?

766 What is the brightest star in the northern hemisphere of the sky?

767 Name the Astronomer Royal who retired at the end of 1971.

768 Which one of these bodies moves round the Sun in a retrograde direction: Encke's Comet, Pluto, the Earth, Vesta, Halley's Comet, Venus?

769 Name the nearest naked-eye star to the south celestial pole?

770 In which constellation would you find the star Capella?

771 Name the outermost of the five satellites of the planet Uranus.

772 Who was the discoverer of Bennett's Comet?

773 Where in the sky would you find Pleione?

774 What is the name of the largest asteroid?

775 Which of the following types of reflectors gives a naturally erect image: Newtonian, Gregorian, Cassegrain?

776 A modern English amateur astronomer has discovered four comets and three novae. He lives near Peterborough. What is his name?

777 Two German observers compiled the first really good map of the Moon in the 1830s. One was Johann Von Madler, who was the other?

778 In what sea would you look for Archimedes?

779 Which has the higher surface temperature; an S-type star or an O-type star?

780 Name one of the two Australian astronomers who discovered the first radio star.

French Literature
Set by Ronald S. Kirkman

781 What is the name of the miser in Molière's play
L'Avare?

782 With which French Romantic poet is the Lac du
Bourget in Savoy particularly associated?

783 Which was the only comedy written by Jean
Racine?

784 Who is the hero of Stendhal's novel *Le Rouge et
le Noir*?

785 What is the name of the village near Geneva where
Voltaire lived for almost twenty years?

786 Which comedy by Jean Anouilh was adapted into
English by Christopher Fry under the title *Ring
Round the Moon*?

787 Bizet's famous opera *Carmen* is based on a short
story of the same name by a nineteenth-century
French novelist. Who was this writer?

788 Who is the principal character in Henri Troyat's
novel *La Tête sur les Epaules*?

789 Whilst awaiting execution Chenier wrote a number
of satirical and political poems. What is their
collective title?

790 The first and third parts of Balzac's *Illusions
Perdues* are set in the same provincial town. What
is this town?

791 In 1964 a French philosopher and writer refused
the Nobel prize for literature. Who is he?

792 Roger Martin du Gard wrote about a French
bourgeois family. What was the title of this series?

793 Ronsard, Du Bellay, Jodelle, Rémy Belleau, de Baïf, de Tyard and Dorat were all members of a sixteenth-century literary group. What was the group called?

794 The trial in 1906 of Mme Blanche-Henriette Canaby for attempted murder was the basis for a famous novel – which one?

795 Which of André Malraux's novels was based on his experience in the Spanish Civil War?

796 The early novels of André Chamson were concerned with peasant life in an underdeveloped region of France. Which region?

797 Which poet was imprisoned in 1526 for having boasted of eating bacon during Lent?

798 Five Arthurian romances in verse were written by the same author. What is the title of the last of these, the theme of which was the Holy Grail?

799 An author and poet recently elected to the Académie Française has written a series of essays on the natural beauty of rocks and stones. Who is he?

800 *Roman de la Rose* was begun by Guillaume de Lorris and completed by another poet. Who was he?

General Knowledge 12

801 A famous monument was blown up in O'Connell Street, Dublin, in March 1966. To whom was it dedicated?

802 In Greek legend a sculptor and craftsman constructed the labyrinth for Minos. Who was he?

803 His best-known works are *Roderick Random* (1748), *Peregrine Pickle* (1751) and *Humphrey Clinker* (1771). Who was he?

804 A morganatic marriage describes what kind of union?

805 In religion, what is the meaning of the words 'Kyrie Eleison'?

806 A Miss Glover of Norwich invented a system of musical notation, about 1845. What was it called?

807 Brooklyn and Staten Island are connected by the longest and heaviest single span suspension bridge in the world. What is it called?

808 Where was Interpol founded?

809 What is the name of the Roman road which runs between the coast of Devon and Lincoln?

810 The 'Mutiny on the Bounty' is well known, but how many mutinies was Captain Bligh involved in?

811 Arachnida is a word used to describe spiders. What is the origin of this word?

812 Britain has only one woman Professor of Physics, who is she?

813 Tolstoy's *War and Peace* has been adapted as an opera. Who is the composer?

814 Who was Alexander the Great's general who took over the government of Egypt when Alexander died?

815 Over which kingdom do King Tupou IV and Queen Mata'aho reign?

816 Alessandro di Mariano Filipepi who was born about 1444, the son of a tanner, is remembered by another name. What name?

817 What are the 'Royal Peculiars'?

818 What was the result of the Saar plebiscite in 1935?

819 Born in Paris in 1908, she won the Prix Goncourt with her novel *The Mandarins*. Who is she?

820 What were the followers of John Wycliffe, the religious reformer, called?

Science Fiction

Set by Tom Shippey

821   In which novel was it the job of the 'fireman' to burn books; as the hero says 'Monday burn Millay, Wednesday Whitman, Friday Faulkner'?

822   What was 'The Seldon Plan' described in the trilogy *Foundation, Foundations and Empire, Second Foundation*?

823   In which novel are 'the Conservationists' an outlawed political party?

824   Who betrayed Duke Leto Atreidea to the Harkonnens?

825   John Carter the Earthman was 'the Warlord of Barsoom', what did he do with a 'thoat'?

826   Of which classic short story are these the first words, 'Put down that wrench'?

827   What have the following novels in common: Brian Aldiss's *Non-Stop*, Harry Harrison's *Captive Universe*, Robert Heinlein's *Orphans of the Sky*, E. C. Tubb's *The Space-born*?

828   Samuel Delany's *Nova* is explicitly presented as the re-handling of an ancient myth. Which one?

829   What is the easiest way of telling a 'slan' from a normal human being?

830   In James Blish's *Earthmen Come Home* series, one of the two inventions necessary to permit travel between the stars was the 'anti-agathic' drugs which enormously increase the human life-span. What was the other?

831   Name two weapons or devices used by the Martians in H. G. Wells's *The War of the Worlds*.

832 What was the message that Salo carried from Tralfamadore in the Small Magellanic Cloud to Titan?

833 A famous novel has been written about a society in which most people have the ability to teleport for a 'jaunte'. Name the novel.

834 In what world did Ransom the philologist learn about war? Give its name in English and Old Solar.

835 What is the best-known sign of insanity in the race known to men as 'Pierson's puppeteers'?

836 In which work does the following appear: Hal 9000?

837 Isaac Asimov invented the Three Laws of Robotics in his stories. What was the first law?

838 Who is the author of *The Drowned World*?

839 Who are the players in 'the game of rat and dragon' in the book of that name?

840 In Jack Vance's *Star King* series, Kirth Gersen is committed to vengeance on the five outlaw-leaders known as the Demon Princes. Name two of them.

TOM SHIPPEY: Lecturer at the University of Birmingham.

Spanish and South American Ethnology

Set by Professor J. C. J. Metford

841 Who, after Franco's death, has been nominated to become King and Chief of State?

842 He ranks as an important Spanish painter, but in fact he was not born in Spain. Who was he?

843 What popular dance originated in Argentina?

844 What in history was known as the Spanish Main?

845 A state of war existed between the US and Spain on 21 April 1898, in connection with what?

846 What was the name of the Spanish explorer who discovered the Mississippi River?

847 What, in the ancient world, were the Pillars of Hercules?

848 Between 1808-1821 the Portuguese Royal Family ruled Portugal from where?

849 Which treaty gave Britain official possession of Gibraltar?

850 One Spanish epic poem survives almost in its complete form, what is it called?

851 What is Mestizo Music?

852 Name the main technological achievement prevalent in the Old World which was absent from the New.

853 Which animals were herded by the ancient peoples of the Andes?

854 What was the *Popal Vuh*?

855 What is the oldest dated monument in the New World?

856 Where is Tiahuanaco?

857 What was the Indian name for the plumed serpent god?

858 What was the language spoken by the Incas?

859 Who were the Zipa and the Zaque?

860 Who were Xochipilli, Huitzilophoctli and Tlaloc?

Professor J. C. J. METFORD, M.A.: Head of Department of Spanish and Portuguese, Bristol University.

Money, Money, Money

Set by William Keegan

861 It is said that you can buy everything at Harrods. Who paid £40 million for Harrods in 1959?

862 Who delivered the Budget Speech in 1853?

863 Roughly, how much was a 1914 pound worth in 1971?

864 How many countries in 1944 were signatories to the original draft of the Articles of Agreement of the International Monetary Fund?

865 In 1810 which City of London institution's leading members were accused of 'absenting themselves in September, October and November to avoid winter risks'?

866 Who introduced super-tax?

867 Which company started the system of travellers' cheques in 1891?

868 Of which economist was it said that he 'conquered England as completely as the Holy Inquisition conquered Spain'?

869 Which economic law has been summarised as 'supply creates its own demand'?

870 Which famous bank collapsed in London in 1890?

871 When did Britain go off the gold standard?

872 'Our power has brought us into touch with Ambassadors', the chairman said in 1875. Whose Chairman?

873 What was the average rate of interest on UK long term bonds in 1946?

874 From what date were joint stock banks permitted to operate within a radius of 65 miles of London?

875 In 1870-1913, during the heyday of British investment overseas, by far the greater proportion of UK capital exports went into what?

876 During how many years between 1960 and 1970 inclusive did Britain have a visible trade surplus with the rest of the world?

877 Who said: 'Believing that fundamental conditions of the country are sound . . . my son and I have for some days been purchasing sound common stocks'?

878 On the West Coast of America during the Civil War years of 1860-1864 average price levels changed hardly at all. How much did they change in the rest of the Union?

879 Two major powers were not on the gold standard in 1880. Austria-Hungary was one of them; which was the other?

880 The US Government spent between 47 and 50 billion dollars on Lend-Lease aid during and after World War II. What proportion went to the British Empire?

WILLIAM KEEGAN of *The Financial Times.*

General Knowledge 13

881 Which English composer wrote the *Fantasia on a theme of Thomas Tallis*?

882 What shape is the large DNA molecule?

883 The stalk of a plant which originated in China and the far East is used for cooking. What is its name?

884 What poet wrote about 'Flannan Isle'?

885 Giovanni Antonio Canal was born in Venice in 1697. What is he remembered for?

886 They were nicknamed The Bald, The Fat, The Simple, The Fair, The Wise. Who were they?

887 What was the name of Hitler's wife?

888 What is the name of the highest civil decoration that can be awarded in France?

889 The harbour of Rio de Janeiro is dominated by a mountain, what is its name?

890 There is a very famous modern chapel in Ronchamp in France, who was the architect?

891 Which American state has the same name as one of the Russian Soviet Republics?

892 What was the name given to the event that involved a group of anarchists, one of them known as Peter the Painter?

893 What are 'Splendour', 'Mirth', and 'Good Cheer', collectively known as?

894 She was the only female member of the BMA for nearly twenty years. Who was she?

895 *Rule Britannia* was written by James Thomson; who set it to music?

896 Which French King was crowned in the cathedral at Reims with the help of Joan of Arc?

897 It was founded by Robert Tyre Jones on the Augusta Course. What was?

898 Who cut the Gordian Knot?

899 What is the county town of Lanarkshire?

900 When the Conservative Party were known as Tories, what were the chief opposition known as?

Answers

General Knowledge 1

1 Sir Barnes Wallis. He also designed the R100 airship, the Wellington bomber, the swing-wing aircraft.

2 Lutine. The bell comes from HMS Lutine, a 32-gun frigate wrecked in 1799 off the Dutch coast. It was carrying money and bullion insured at Lloyd's. It hangs in the Underwriting Room at Lloyd's in London, and is rung to draw attention to the announcement of news items. One stroke means that bad news will follow. Two strokes indicates that the following news is good.

3 1935

4 Roman Catholics, under the Catholic Emancipation Act of 1829. They were allowed to sit in Parliament and hold any public office, except Lord Chancellor or Lord Lieutenant of Ireland, provided they took an oath denying the Pope's right to interfere in British affairs.

5 Dame Ninette de Valois.

6 Daniel Defoe. English novelist and political pamphleteer, 1660–1731. He was born in London, and was also author of *Robinson Crusoe, Moll Flanders* etc.

7 Ceres.

8 Clock Tower and Victoria Tower. The south-western Victoria (or Central) Tower is 336ft high. The Clock Tower (or St Steven's Tower) is 329ft high and contains the clock famous for its $13\frac{1}{2}$-ton bell, Big Ben.

9 Dr Konrad Adenauer (1876–1967). He was founder and Chairman of the Christian Democratic Party (or Union) (1946–1956), and Chancellor of the West German Federal Republic.

10 Arnold Schönberg (1874–1951). The system is illustrated in Schönberg's Suite for Piano, Opus 25, 1923, and was adopted by his pupils Alban Berg and Anton Webern.

11 35 imperial gallons or 42 US gallons.

12 A diamond (the Hope Diamond), which at 44·4 carats is one of the largest known diamonds, and was probably part of a 112½-carat stone found in the Killmur mine, Golconda, India.

13 Because they believe that the Dalai Lama is re-incarnated in this way.

14 South-east Asia. (Indonesia, includes Bali). The Indonesian (and Siamese) orchestra. A full Gamelan orchestra is a powerful producer of rich and varied tones and depends largely on percussion for its effects, using instruments of the marimba, xylophone and gong type.

15 Harold Pinter.

16 Swimming. From the Latin *natantem, natare*, to swim.

17 Tom Rakewell. The Rake occurs in the well-known series of pictures by Hogarth. Stravinsky's last opera, *The Rake's Progress*, was based on these pictures.

18 Filling the house with invited guests on complimentary tickets.

19 Faust, or Doctor Faustus.

20 Katmandu.

Twentieth-century English Literature

21 *Ulysses* (by James Joyce).

22 *To Let*.

23 Borneo. Borneo is part of the Malay Archipelago and consists of part of Indonesia and Brunei and part of the Federation of Malaysia.

24 Peacock. *The White Peacock*, 1911.

25 *Howards End* (E. M. Forster, 1910).

26 *The Loom of Youth* (1917).

27 They are sisters in G. B. Shaw's play *Heartbreak House* (1919).

28 *Brighton Rock* (Graham Greene, 1938).

29 John Masefield.

30 W. B. Yeats.

31 He invented Tono-Bungay, a patent medicine (H. G. Wells *Tono-Bungay* 1909).

32 *Back to Methusalah* (1921).

33 *Under Milk Wood* by Dylan Thomas (1954).

34 *Clea.* By Lawrence Durrell. The titles of the four books in his *The Alexandria Quartet.*

35 David John Moore Cornwell, who wrote under the pseudonym, John Le Carré.

36 *Lord of the Flies* by William Golding (1954).

37 Osbert and Sacheverell.

38 Richard Hillary.

39 A wandering music-hall troupe (Oakroyal, Sam Oglethorpe, Mr and Mrs Tarvin, the Dulner family).

40 Shangri-la.

National Flags Past and Present

41 The flags of the United Nations, of Great Britain, Nepal and India in that order.

42 This was the first emblem of the Confederate States in the American Civil War. It was superseded by the Southern Cross Flag because its resemblance to the Stars and Stripes proved confusing in battle.

43 The Moslem regions used a Red Crescent flag, and Iran uses a variant of its national emblem, a Red Lion grasping a sword. All three emblems are borne on a white field.

44 There are nine horizontal stripes, alternately blue and white, to represent the nine symbols of the Greek slogan *Eleutheria a thanatos*, 'Freedom or death'.

45 'There is no god but God and Mohammed is the Prophet of God' – the Moslem declaration of faith.

46 The legend was that a wandering people might make their home where they saw an eagle alighting on a cactus and bearing a serpent in its beak, and this emblem now appears on the National Flag of Mexico.

47 Miniature Russian flags were scattered on the surface of the Moon by the *Luna 2* in 1959, and the Stars and Stripes was raised above it by Armstrong and Aldrin in 1969.

48 The state flag of Hawaii, the flag also bears eight horizontal stripes, white, red, blue, white, red, blue, white, red.

49 They were at first orange, white and blue, the family colours of the Price of Orange, but the orange stripe was replaced by red to give greater visibility at sea.

50 The reverse of the Standard of the Emperor of Ethiopia.

51 The national emblem of a wreath encircling a hammer and a pair of dividers is placed on the horizontal tricolour of black, red and gold.

52 The relationship between Argentina and Uruguay marked by the use of this emblem, the sudden appearance of this emblem through the clouds when these regions won their independence being regarded as a good omen.

53 Those of Norway and of Great Britain respectively, taken there by Amundsen and Scott.

54 By patterns of horizontal or vertical stripes or by a slight variation of the hammer and sickle emblem.

55 The national flag of Iceland, which also bears a red St George's Cross edged with white on a blue field. However it has no diagonal stripes and the vertical arm of the cross is somewhat nearer the hoist.

56 Malawi and Antigua display the rising sun; British Columbia bears the setting sun, which in that area is seen over the Pacific.

57 A hand emerging from a cloud, mailed in armour and brandishing a sword with the motto *Vince aut Mourir*, 'Victory or death'. A somewhat similar emblem but with a different motto, appeared on a Parliamentary Cavalry Standard in the British Civil War.

58 Edward III (and subsequent monarchs) not only claimed the throne of France but showed that he regarded this as the most important part of his realm by placing the Lilies in the first quarter of his standard. At the Union of England and Scotland, Queen Anne regarded this United Kingdom as the most important part of her realm and placed the emblems of both countries in the first quarter, relegating the French Lilies to the second. George III removed them from the flag in 1802 to show that by the Treaty of Amiens he had relinquished all claim to rule France.

59 That formerly used by New Zealand and now the house flag of the Shaw Savill and Albion Co Ltd. Originally it was the emblem of the United Tribes of New Zealand.

· 60 It was the Governor's flag of the British North Borneo Company which administered Sabah, formerly a British Protectorate. It displayed a red lion rampant on a small gold disc at the centre of the Union Jack.

General Knowledge 2

61 Sir Alexander Korda.

62 His authorised translation of the Bible. The version of 1611 arose from a recommendation made at Hampton Court Conference 1604 by Dr Reynolds, president of Corpus Christi College, Oxford.

63 Centaur.

64 Ormolu. Derived from the French, *or moulu*, literally ground gold.

65 Orion. A conspicuous and easily recognisable constellation near the equator. Betelgeuse is the brightest star in the constellation.

66 Mrs Bandaranaike, Prime Minister of Ceylon or Shri Lanka.

67 The Sikh religion. It is kept in the Temple of Amritsar.

68 A skull (the Piltdown man). At the time, 1908–12, it was thought that a new genus of man had been found. In fact the skull was made up from ordinary homo sapiens and modern ape bones. This carefully planned hoax which gulled most of the experts was exposed in 1953 by Weimer Oakley and Legros Clerk in the bulletin of the British Museum.

69 A lighthouse – the first pharos. The Pharos, a tower of white marble c. 400ft high built by Ptolemy II Philadelphus at Alexandria about 280 BC. Demolished by an earthquake in the fourteen century, it was usually included among the seven wonders of the world in ancient times.

70 The Republic of Upper Volta.

71 Five. (St Hugh's, St Anne's, St Hilda's, Lady Margaret Hall, and Somerville.) There are 32 for men.

72 President John F. Kennedy, in his inaugural address.

73 The Order of the Garter. Motto is 'Honi soit qui mal y pense'.

74 A massive stalagmite in Wookey Hole caves, Somerset. It is said by legend to be a petrified woman.

75 The Liberal Party.

76 James Abbott McNeil Whistler (1834–1903). The portrait of his mother is also known as *Arrangement in Grey and Black*.

77 Stilton.

78 A sculptor and king of Cyprus who fell in love with his own statue of Aphrodite. He is supposed to have persuaded the goddess Aphrodite through his earnest prayers to give life to the statue – which he married.

79 A kind of glazed and ornamented pottery supposed to have been brought to Europe from Majorca in the fifteenth century.

80 The liver.

Grand Opera

81 *The Bartered Bride* (Smetana).

82 Stravinsky.

83 Works – Latin – opus, the plural being opera.

84 Beaumarchais: *The Barber of Seville*.

85 Alexander Pushkin.

86 Munich, 1869.

87 Dame Nellie Melba.

88 Gounod's *Faust*.

89 Peri's *Dafni* (produced in Florence in 1597).

90 In Venice (Teatro San Cassiano, 1637).

91 La Scala Milan. On the site of a church founded by Regine Della Scala in the fourteenth century. Not Covent Garden which stands on the site of a garden.

92 Three.

93 1,003.

94 They stood for 'Viva vittorio Emmanuele re
D'Italia' at the time of the Risorgimento,
proclaiming Victor Emmanuel King of all Italy.

95 Nine, the eight Walküres plus Brünnhilde.

96 Wagner's name for the covered orchestral pit at
Bayreuth.

97 The Fieldmarschallin's Uncle mentioned in act one
of *Der Rosenkavalier*.

98 *The Tales of Hoffman* which are related while a
performance of *Don Giovanni* takes place at an
adjoining theatre.

99 June Bronhill. Her stage name is a contraction of
Broken Hill. The residents of this Australian town
where she was born helped to pay for her to go to
London in 1952.

100 The name by which the Duke of Mantua passed
himself off when wooing Gilda in *Rigoletto*.

Astronomy 1

101 Pluto. Pluto was discovered photographically in
1930 and announced in March at Lowell
Observatory, Flagstaff, Arizona, USA – although
its existence had been suggested many years before.

102 A gap separating two of Saturn's rings. The
division is seen as a dark band 2,500 miles wide
separating the two other rings of Saturn, ring A
and ring B.

103 It would break up into fragments. The Roche limit
is a distance equal to 2·44 times the radius of the
planet from its centre. If a moon should approach
closer than this distance, it is shattered into
fragments by the planet's gravitational field.
Saturn's rings were probably formed in this way.
Our moon is 60 radii away so there is no likelihood
of the moon shattering. The limit does not apply
to artificial satellites, which are held together by
their structural cohesion.

104 Jupiter.

105 Ten. The tenth, Janus, was discovered in 1966.

106 55 to 60 days, or to be exact, 58½ days.

107 A star that produces *regular* pulses of radio waves. The pulses are emitted at regular intervals varying from 1/30 second up to 3 seconds. Some pulsars also produce regular pulses of X-rays and light waves.

108 Venus.

109 William Herschel (1738–1822). Discovered 1781.

110 Saturn, which has a density lower than water and could float on one of our seas. Except that it is 763 times the volume of the earth.

111 John Flamsteed (1646–1719) made accurate observations of the moon that helped Newton to formulate the laws of gravitation.

112 The Steady State Theory.

113 On the moon. They are all lunar craters.

114 It will be exactly opposite to the sun in our sky.

115 Tycho Brahe.

116 Mare Humorum.

117 Messier 31 and the Andromeda Spiral.

118 They indicate the official sequence of the spectral types of stars.

119 It has an eccentric orbit.

120 R Coronae Borealis.

General Knowledge 3

121 The Liffey.

122 Lines joining places with the same temperature.

123 The Olympic Games. The Ninth Games, at Amsterdam in 1928, when new attractions were the five track and field events as well as gymnastics, fencing, swimming and diving for women.

124 Tsaritsyn (until 1925), on the Volga, renamed to commemorate its defence by Stalin in 1917 against the White Russians. Stalin died in 1953 and in 1962 the name was changed to Volgograd.

125 Alexandrine.

126 Lanfranc.

127 The Delta Plan. Approved in 1959, it is the largest flood control project in Dutch history.

128 A word formed by the first letter of each line of a poem or other composition. If the final letters also form a word it is a double acrostic. If the middle letters also it is a triple acrostic.

129 Wild cherries.

130 An ancient Herald's Wand carried by a Greek or Roman herald. Also the fabled wand carried by Hermes or Mercury as the messenger of the gods; usually represented with two serpents twined round it.

131 Austerlitz, fought on 2 December 1805. The emperors were Napoleon, Francis II of Austria, and Alexander I of Russia.

132 Nowhere – literally, not place (ou = not, topos = place).

133 Niccolo Machiavelli (1469–1527), an Italian statesman and author. Machiavellian: 'pertaining to, or characteristic of Machiavelli or his alleged principles – practising duplicity especially in statecraft – astute cunning'.

134 The discovery of the Dead Sea Scrolls in 1947.

135 Westmorland.

136 CD.

137 Attila. The Huns were an Asiatic race that swept over Europe, and were defeated at Chalons-sur-Marne in 451. The death of Attila in 453 terminated the Empire.

138 A *chiton*.

139 Gunwale.

140 Lily of the valley.

Classical Mythology

141 Tending his father's sheep on Mount Ida.

142 Ten years.

143 He was shot in the heel by an arrow sent by either Paris or Apollo.

144 He broke the condition not to look back on the way up.

145 Deucalion and Pyrrha.

146 Alcestis, wife of Admetus.

147 So that Atlas might be free to fetch the apples of the Hesperides.

148 Helen of Troy.

149 Phaedra, wife of Theseus, step-mother of Hippolytus.

150 Lion, goat, and serpent.

151 Hermes was god of both.

152 Persephone (Kore).

153 For giving man fire and/or for cheating the gods of the better parts of sacrificial animals.

154 Man. (The question: What is it that walks on four legs in the morning, on two at noon, on three in the evening?)

155 They had killed them.

156 VIIa.

157 Heinrich Schliemann.

158 To spread the knowledge of corn-growing.

159 The site of an ancient sanctuary of the Muses near Mount Olympus in Thessaly.

160 Cow or Ox-ford since Zeus' love Io swam across in the shape of a cow.

History of Music 1550-1900

161 Largo. But scored 'Larghetto e piano'.

162 Comic Opera. In Italian 'opera buffa'.

163 Bach's two sets of twenty-four preludes and fugues in all twenty-four keys, sometimes known as 'The Well-tempered Clavier' or '*Das wohltemperirte Clavier*'.

164 Purcell's *Dido and Aeneas*.

165 It was a serenade.

166 Galliard.

167 Funeral March Sonata.

168 William Boyce.

169 'Chopsticks'.

170 *Cox and Box*.

171 Leonora.

172 Stephen Collins Foster.

173 Songs without words (Lieder ohne Worte).

174 Because the fourth of the five movements is a set of variations on his song *The Trout* (*Die Forelle*).

175 Dresden.

176 Three string quartets known as the Rasumovsky Quartets (Op. 59 in F, E minor and C).

177 Dublin (at the New Music Hall).

178 Pasticcio.

179 Ceylon (although the characters are Indians).

180 Alphonse Daudet.

General Knowledge 4

181 Aeolus. The personifications of the winds were: Notus was the south or south-west winds. Boreas the north wind, Eurus the south-east wind and Zephyrus the west wind.

182 Presidency of the USA.

183 In law, Assault is threatening to strike, or striking and missing the target, while Battery is actually hitting the target (person).

184 Having a Turkish bath. The original name was hummum.

185 Greta Garbo.

186 The end of the World. He is usually credited with the founding of the Advertists, a Protestant sect.

187 Blaise Pascal (1623–62).

188 John Crome (1768–1821).

189 He was, and is, the youngest recipient of the VC At the time he was fifteen years old.

190 Ivan the Terrible.

191 The eider duck breeds there. Their down is used to stuff quilts etc. They also breed in the Hebrides and Donegal.

192 Sergei Pavlovich Diaghilev (1872–1929).

193 The circumnavigation of the world.

194 The Loire. 625 miles long, it flows from the Cévennes Mountains to the Atlantic.

195 Whale Shark. It grows to a length of 40 ft and weighs up to 20 tons.

196 Campanology. The term covers the whole of the knowledge of bells, theoretical, historical, etc.

197 Sir Henry Percy (1364–1403). Son of Earl of Northumberland, helped Henry Bolingbroke to depose Richard II. Popular nickname given to Sir Henry Percy because of his fiery temper and zeal in border warfare. Shakespeare used the pseudonym in the two parts of Henry IV.

198 Lord Annan, Provost of University College, London. Subject was 'What are Universities for Anyway?'

199 A boundary the crossing of which means that one becomes committed. The Rubicon was a stream limiting Caesar's province and crossed by him before war with Pompey.

200 Jean Anouilh, the French dramatist born in 1910.

British Politics Since 1900

201 1931. National Government supporters 554, Labour 52, others 9. Clear National Government majority 493. The position of two or three MP's is arguable but the answer must lie in the 485–501 region.

202 September/October 1903 in protest against Joseph Chamberlain's suggestion of ending free trade.

203 'The House of Lords is not the watchdog of the constitution. It is Mr Balfour's poodle.' Lloyd George said this in 1909, quoted in Roy Jenkins' book *Mr Balfour's Poodle*.

204 Three. In 1910 (13 Feb–28 Nov); 1922–3 (20 Nov–16 Nov), 11 months 27 days with the elections 12½ months apart; and 1924 (8 Jan–9 Oct).

205 Asquith, from 5 April 1908–6 Dec 1916, 8 years 8 months. Others in the list are Macmillan, 10 Jan 1957–Oct 1963, 6 years 9 months; and Lloyd George, 6 Dec 1916–23 Oct 1922, 5 years 10 months. Lord Salisbury was PM for thirteen years in all and his last premiership, 1895–1902, lasted seven years and one month.

206 Prime Minister (May 1940–July 1945). Not Chancellor of the Exchequer, Oct 1924–May 1929.

207 The Vesting Date under the Iron and Steel Act 1949 was January 1951. The industry was, of course, de-nationalised by the Iron and Steel Act 1953. The Vesting Date under the Iron and Steel Act 1967 was 28 July 1967.

208 Under the Ministers of the Crown Act, 1937.

209 Harold Wilson, as President of the Board of Trade in November 1948.

210 R. A. Butler referring to Sir Anthony Eden in December 1955.

211 Stanley Baldwin, speaking of the Empire Crusade Campaign of the Press Lords, Beaverbrook and Rothermere, during the Westminster by-election of March 1931.

212 September 1935.

213 Frank Cousins, Oct 1964–July 1966.

214 In 1958 by the Life Peerage Act. There were a few Law Lords before that.

215 Harold Macmillan as Chancellor of the Exchequer, in his Budget of 17 April 1956.

216 As a result of protests against the Hoare-Laval pact over Abyssinia (on 18 December 1935).

217 Anthony Wedgwood Benn, whose efforts not to become Viscount Stansgate led to the passage of the Peerage Act 1963 which came into effect on 1 August 1963. Sir Alec Douglas Home and Quintin Hogg renounced their peerages in October 1963, Wedgwood Benn never used his title.

218 Harold Wilson coined the phrase in Feb 1970 to refer to what he saw as the Tory attitudes typified at the meeting of Conservative leaders to discuss policy at Selsdon Park Hotel, Croydon, on 31 January.

219 Sir Stafford Cripps' devaluation of 18 Sept 1949 when the dollar exchange rate was cut from $4·03 to $2·80.

220 A Government Committee under Lord Fulton which considered the structure and functioning of the Civil Service and reported in July 1968. Among the recommendations that were implemented were the setting up of the Civil Service Department and the abolition of many of the existing barriers between Civil Service grades.

English Costume

221 Lincoln (it was known as Lincoln green).

222 Balls of mixed aromatic substances carried for perfume or as a guard against infection (the term was sometimes used just for the case).

223 Mrs Amelia Jenks Bloomer (she became famous in 1851 for her 'Turkish pantaloons' although she was probably not the first to wear this garment. She advocated their use in her journal 'Lily'. They were especially recommended for cycling).

224 Wooden sandals or overshoes mounted on iron rings to raise the foot above the wet ground (the meaning has changed slightly and come to mean wooden overshoes with a thick wooden sole).

225 Large hat trimmed with flowers or print dress with flower pattern (the first is better and much more frequently used as a 'Dolly Varden'. Dolly Varden was a character who wore these clothes in *Barnaby Rudge*).

226 A Blücher is a low boot and a Wellington is a high boot.

227 A one-piece woman's overdress with a waist and an open skirt.

228 The tail, or streamer from a man's bonnet that hung over his shoulder, or the long tail of a graduate's hood in early academic costume (fifteenth century).

229 As a handkerchief – that is what it was.

230 A hard low-crowned felt hat (Americans call them 'derbies' or 'derby hats').

231 An opera or crush hat.

232 Grey woollen plaids worn in Southern Scotland.

233 Breeches. 'Spanish slops' were loose baggy breeches and 'Venetians' were padded breeches.

234 A large wired stand-up collar. It was worn in Elizabethan times, and it is correct to say 'Queen Elizabeth wore a whisk'. By Pepys' time it had become a neckerchief.

235 Coloured satin that was crimson in the shadows and pink in the highlights.

236 Sugar-loaf.

237 That the traveller had been on a pilgrimage to the Holy Land, which entitled him to be known as a 'palmer'.

238 From the 'sabots' or wooden clogs worn by peasants in the days of the Normans. The French and Dutch peasants wore 'sabots'. Sabotage has derived from the damage done by French peasants to the crops of their lords which they trampled if they thought they were being treated unjustly.

239 A Jewish person.

240 A deep falling collar attached to the top of a low-necked dress.

Words

241 Any word that reads the same backwards as forwards (e.g. Anna).

242 An argument (or form of reasoning) comprising two premises sharing a common term and a conclusion that must be true if the premises are true (first classified by Aristotle).

243 Latin – *lingua*, meaning tongue.

244 According to the value.

245 Simple arrangement of words in a meaningful order.

246 Words that descend from a common ancestor, e.g. chase and catch which come from the Latin *captare*.

247 'Cabriolet' (originally meant leap or caper).

248 The treatment of diseases with small quantities of drugs that produce the symptoms similar to those of the disease (like cures like).

249 It comes from two Latin words *re*, meaning back or backwards, and *calx*, *calcis*, meaning hoof. The two together in Latin (*recalcitrare*) mean 'to kick back'.

250 A written sign to show changes in sound and pronounciation.

251 Old English after, and mawan, mowing (there is a crop of grass springs up after the first mowing in the summer. When it is cut you reap an aftermath).

252 A newly conceived word that has been generally accepted.

253 From Arabian *hashshashin*, eaters of hashish (original charter-member assassins were a religious sect in Palestine, Moslem fanatics, sworn by their shiekh, 'the old man of the Mountains' to murder all crusaders. When their fervour cooled their leader gave them hashish to drink).

254 The day of the mandate (or commandment) when Christ washed the Disciples' feet (a corruption of the Latin *dies mandati*. First words of an anthem sung on this day in R.C. churches 'Mandatum Novum Do Vobis', 'A New Commandment I give unto you that ye love one another' – Solomon 13, v. 34).

255 Son of the Commandments or one responsible for the Commandments. (Religious ritual and family celebration to commemorate a boy's thirteenth birthday which traditionally is his coming of age and responsibility for fulfilling all the Commandments.)

256 Italian *balla*, ball. Secret voting in early days was done by dropping small balls in an urn or box.

257 'Drink nothing' – an Australian aboriginal word.

258 Latin *candidatus*, white-robed. Romans seeking office had to wear white togas before election day so that voters could recognise them.

259 Latin – *salarium*. Originally salt-money, money given to soldiers for salt or the payment to Roman soldiers given in salt.

260 After John Montagu, fourth Earl of Sandwich (1718–1792). He spent 24 hours on the gaming table without a regular meal and ordered his servant to bring him bread and roast beef. He then put them together and made the first sandwich.

General Knowledge 5

261 Welland Ship Canal.

262 In the Channel Islands. Guernsey and Jersey are Bailiwicks.

263 The seccession of South Carolina which, with ten other Southern States, formed the Confederacy.

264 Archery. The contestants shoot at a small target from a trotting horse.

265 Rudolf Diesel (1858–1913).

266 Irish wolfhound.

267 Henry IV.

268 Forest.

269 Wolfson College, because of a gift of two million pounds from the Wolfson Foundation.

270 Lord Reith.

271 Thomas Cromwell.

272 King Edward VI.

273 Aldous Huxley. *Mortal Coils* a collection of five of Huxley's early short stories which first appeared in 1922.

274 John of Gaunt, in Act 2, Scene 1.

275 During the Boer War. The name was given to centres where Boer civilians were interned by Kitchener from 1900–1902.

276 Jens Otto Krag.

277 John Calvin (1509–64). Founded 'Calvinism', a branch of Protestantism.

278 Gipsy. Hence *Zingaresca*, a gipsy song.

279 A celestial bull was sent to destroy him. The hero was Gilgamesh.

280 Sidney James Webb (1859–1947). He was a founder member of the Fabian Society, and was raised to the Peerage in 1929.

British Moths

281 Silver Y.

282 Elephant Hawk.

283 Because the caterpillar sits in a hunched up attitude similar to that demonstrated in the Egyptian Sphinx.

284 Because it is a good example of industrial melanism and shows natural selection in action. The peppered moth has changed colour to suit conditions. The moths that did not were vulnerable.

285 Burnet moths.

286 Currant moth or Magpie.

287 In a damp cellar in London on the banks of the Thames.

288 Goat moth.

289 The pugs.

290 Emperor moth.

291 Rosy marsh moth.

292 The Burnished Brass.

293 They cannot fly.

294 The moth has no vocal chords but it can produce a squeak by forcing air through its hollow tongue.

295 The caterpillars feed inside the branches or shoots of their food plants.

296 The Footman. For example the *Red-necked Footman.*

297 Moths have an acute sense of smell and males can locate females by scent alone.

298 The Kittens form a separate group; the Sallow, Alder and Poplar Kittens. It is thought that the small caterpillars resemble kittens with their pointed 'ears' and short tails.

299 Completely dark, muggy nights.

300 The wings are covered in white scales which can look ghostlike in the dark.

English Literature

301 Sir Thomas Malory (?–1471) collected and rewrote stories of chivalry for his romance *Le Morte D'Arthur*, published by William Caxton in 1485.

302 Rosalind (*As you like it*).

303 *The Schoolmaster* by Roger Ascham (1515–1568).

304 Earl of Chesterfield (Philip Dormer Stanhope, fourth Earl of Chesterfield). Johnson sent Chesterfield a prospectus of his *Dictionary* and received £10 subscription. Later he claimed he was left waiting in an ante-room when Cibber was admitted. He certainly expected more help from a man who professed to be a patron of literature, and wrote the Earl the famous letter in defence of of men of letters.

305 Joseph Addison (1672–1719).

306 Euphuism. Literary flamboyance demonstrated in *Euphues the Anatomy of Wit* and *Euphues and his England*. John Lyly (1554?–1606) influenced Shakespeare's work.

307 Sir Walter Scott (debts of £130,000 incurred by Ballantyne and Constable).

308 Knutsford in Cheshire. Mrs Elizabeth Gaskell (1810–1865) wrote *Cranford* giving a lively account of village life in the mid-nineteenth century.

309 'Come live with me and be my love' (Marlowe *A Passionate Shepherd to his Love*, Donne *The Bait*).

310 *Joseph Andrews* (it began as a parody but developed its own individuality).

311 *Bleak House* (1853).

312 The name is an anagram of *Nowhere*.

313 United Services College, Westward Ho! In *Stalky & Co* by Rudyard Kipling (1865–1936).

314 Charles Lutwidge Dodgson. The author 'Lewis Carroll' who wrote *Alice in Wonderland*.

315 Sir George Etherege (1633–1693?), author of *The Comical Revenge* etc.

316 Mr W. H. Given in this way in the dedication to Shakespeare's sonnets.

317 Prime Minister of Britain. He was Benjamin Disraeli.

318 *The Life of Samuel Johnson* (by James Boswell, 1740–1795). The meeting took place in 1763.

319 C. Auguste Dupin. He appears in *The Murders in the Rue Morgue* and *The Mystery of Marie Roget*. Edgar Allan Poe (1809–1849) was one of America's greatest poets.

320 Brontë sisters. Charlotte, Emily and Anne.

Tudor History

321 Edward Poynings.

322 Erasmus of Rotterdam.

323 Enclosures (of land especially for pasture, and especially at the expense of the peasantry).

324 Sir Thomas Wyatt.

325 All were burned for their faith, in the time of Mary Tudor.

326 Apprentices rioted against and attacked alien residents. Many were later hanged for taking part.

327 Officially – and probably at least partly – Henry VIII. For his work he was given the title 'Defender of the Faith'.

328 Wednesday was made a Fish Day – though exemptions could be bought.

329 1539, the Act of Six Articles – Henry VIII's Catholic doctrines for his Church of England.

330 Charles Brandon, Duke of Suffolk. (Their descendents were possible claimants to the English throne in later Tudor times.)

331 Printing – he was Caxton's assistant and successor.

332 They were ordered to maintain parish registers of baptisms, marriages and burials – vital evidence for genealogy and the study of local families and population movements.

333 Thomas Howard, fourth Duke of Norfolk, in 1572.

334 A levy on movable property, respectively rural and urban.

335 Sebastian Cabot.

336 A Golden Hind.

337 Consecutive years of deficit to disastrous harvests in a country whose agriculture was still only producing at subsistence level (as a result of bad weather).

338 Nicholas Hilliard.

339 (c) Wolsey the peace-maker; but where he differs from this line it is always in connection with the demands of the King.

340 About 3 million. Russell's estimate is 3·22 million; Cornwall's 2·8 million.

General Knowledge 6

341 The Skylark.

342 Friedrich Wilhelm Nietzsche (1844–1900), the German Philosopher.

343 President Sukarno.

344 Képi.

345 4p.m. to 6p.m. (1600–1800). Second dog-watch runs from 6p.m. to 8p.m.

346 Yeomen of the Guard.

347 Marlene Dietrich.

348 The first submarine. Robert Fulton (1765–1815), was an American engineer born of Irish parents.

349 Ben Travers.

350 To measure electrical resistance of a conductor.

351 Thomas Hardy (1840–1928).

352 A diamond. (Jonker's Diamond). One of the largest known diamonds 44·4 carats, and probably part of 112½-carat stone found in the Killmur mine, Golconda, India.

353 Harrow School. About 1850.

354 Polyvinyl chloride.

355 Rudolf Friml. Czech-American Composer.

356 Improvised mast used in place of one lost or broken.

357 Washington Irving. American writer who created Rip Van Winkle.

358 The Mystery Cat, in *Macavity; The Mystery Cat*, a poem included in *Old Possum's Book of Practical Cats*.

359 John Buchan (1875–1940). Author of *The Thirty Nine Steps; Greenmantle, The Three Hostages, Huntingtower*, and much more.

360 Thomas Alva Edison (1847–1931). He constructed the machine, (gramophone or phonograph) with the intention that it should be used as a dictating machine.

Assissinations and Murders

361 Four. Lincoln, Garfield, McKinley, and Kennedy.

362 Spencer Perceval (in 1812).

363 In the lobby of the House of Commons.

364 *Our American Cousin.*

365 Englebert Dollfuss.

366 John Felton.

367 Memphis, Tennessee.

368 Jack Ruby.

369 King Alexander I.

370 Sophie.

371 Sirhan Bishara Sirhan.

372 Mohandas Karamchand Gandhi.

373 Fly papers, which two servants said she soaked in water to extract the arsenic.

374 In the Hammersmith Palace of Varieties.

375 Edith Thompson.

376 John Reginald Halliday Christie. He was hanged in 1953.

377 Ruth Ellis, in 1955.

378 Not proven.

379 That Podola was suffering from hysteria amnesia. He could not remember what had happened.

380 Sir Bernard (or Dr) Spilsbury.

Visual Arts

381 1937.

382 John Piper (1903–).

383 Reg Butler (1913–) *The Unknown Political Prisoner*.

384 Le Corbusier. Professional name of Charles-Edouard Jeanneret (1887–1965). He developed the international style.

385 S. W. Hayter, who in the 1920s established an experimental school of gravure and printmaking.

386 A painting on a wood panel of Christ or the Holy Family, or of the angels and saints.

387 The Virgin.

388 The Cathedral of Montreal near Palermo in Sicily.

389 Fernand Leger (1881–1955), French artist who developed a distinctive style that reflects modern technology.

390 Jack Smith.

391 He was the teacher of the sculptors in a show of that name at the Whitechapel Art Gallery.

392 Robert Rauschenberg (1925–). A founder of the pop art school. He calls his works *combine paintings* or *combions*.

393 Hagia Sophia (The Holy Wisdom).

394 Robert Norris.

395 Joseph Beuys.

396 Torcello Cathedral.

397 Jasper Johns.

398 The Transfiguration.

399 843.

400 A Byzantine manuscript painted about the year AD 700.

History of Aeronautics

401 Louis Blériot. 25 July 1909.

402 The boomerang. Not the arrow which is not airborne aerodynamically and is only aerodynamically stabilised by its feathers.

403 Pilotless hot-air balloons carrying bombs released by time-fuses. Sent over by the Austrians in 1849.

404 Blanchard and Jeffries. The flight was made in a hydrogen balloon on 7 January 1785 from near Dover Castle and ended in the forest of Guines, near Calais. The pilot was the Frenchman Jean Pierre Blanchard and his passenger was the American physician Dr John Jeffries, who paid for the trip.

405 An Antoinette monoplane in July 1909. Hubert Latham took off from Sangatte, near Calais, on 19 July 1909 in the Antoinette IV fitted with ailerons and designed by Leon Levavasseur who also designed the Antoinette engine which powered it. The machine suffered engine failure when seven or eight miles out and had to ditch in the Channel, Latham being rescued and the machine salvaged.

406 The D.H. Moth. Designed by Geoffrey de Havilland.

407 The Heinkel *HE 178*. First flew in 1939 in Germany. The engine was designed by Dr Hans von Chain and the machine made its first flight on 27 August 1939. The engine was a centrifugal flow turbojet.

408 By fitting stub-wings. The first test vehicle to be fitted with such surfaces was the A-7.

409 Supermarine S6 seaplane.

410 Lieutenant T. E. Selfridge (who was killed) or Orville Wright (who was injured). Lieutenant Thomas E. Selfridge, US Signal Corps, was flying with Orville Wright in the military acceptance trials at Fort Myer in the Wright Type A. A blade of the starboard propeller split and put it out of balance, causing it to flatten, lose thrust and 'wave'; this in turn led to the shaft working the outrigger loose until the propeller was waving right out of its arc and cut through a bracing wire to twin rear rudders; the rudders then collapsed and the machine went into a dive and crashed, killing Selfridge and injuring Orville Wright.

411 The Antoinette. Designed by Leon Levavasseur. First the 50h.p. then the 100h.p. The engine and the monoplane Levavasseur also designed were both called Antoinette after Antoinette Gastambide daughter of the head of the firm.

412 In Germany – between various German cities. Five Zeppelins carried over 35,000 passengers, without a fatality, between various German cities.

413 Jaques Garnerin, in 1797 in Paris. Garnerin was taken up by a balloon and cast off from a height of about 3,000 feet. The parachute was ribbed like an umbrella and Garnerin went up with it closed. It opened as it fell and he came down safely but feeling sick from the parachute pendulating badly due to lack of porosity of the fabric.

414 To cut the neck-line and let the envelope float up into the top of the net and act as a primitive parachute. This first happened with Coxwell, Gypson and two others in Gypson's balloon in 1847, Coxwell realising what to do and doing it.

415 Wilbur Wright. Wright flew this first circle on the Wright Flyer II at the Huffman Prairie (or Pasture) near Dayton, Ohio on 20 September 1904. It was witnessed and described by Amos I. Root.

416 Because they remained unpublished until late in the nineteenth century when aeronautical thought was too advanced to be influenced. The first significant publication of da Vinci's work came with an illustrated article by Hureau de Villeneuve in the French aeronautical periodical *L'Aeronaute* in 1874.

417 They were allowed to hinge freely *upwards* but prevented by wires from moving downwards. He adopted this arrangement after he had crashed one of his gliders. He believed that the nose-dive (into which it went) was caused by the pressure of the air on his then rigid tail-plane pushing up the tail-unit and putting the nose down.

418 By warping (twisting) the wings. The device was invented by the Wright brothers.

419 The Wright brothers gliders of 1901 and 1902. Illustrations of these were shown to European pioneers, particularly by Chanute in Paris in 1903.

420 Robert Esnault-Pelterie on his Wright type glider in 1904.

General Knowledge 7

421 The three gorgons.

422 Charlotte Corday, on 13 July 1793.

423 Egypt. The Temple of Amun is surrounded by the modern village of Karnak.

424 Henry Purcell.

425 Like poles repel, unlike poles attract; or, the force between the poles is proportional to their strength, and inversely proportional to the square of the distance between them.

426 When two organisms live together and both derive mutual benefit from the association. An example is the symbiosis of a pea-plant and the bacteria which lives in its roots, or the fungus and alga composing lichens.

427 Between the fore legs of a horse. A leather strap – one end fastened to the girth of a horse, the other to the bit.

428 Herefordshire.

429 Mormon, or Church of Jesus Christ of Latter Day Saints.

430 John Wilkes. (1727–1797.) Put in Tower in 1763 for criticising King George III's speech.

431 Cardinal Wolsey in 1525.

432 Holy writings of the Jewish Scriptures.

433 The Hapsburgs. The German is 'Habsburgs'.

434 Laurie Lee, in his autobiography *As I Walked Out One Midsummer Morning*.

435 Field Marshall Paul Von Hindenburg (1925–34).

436 The Potteries. (Arnold Bennett's 'Five Towns'.) There were actually six (Fenton) but he used poetic licence in naming five, and gave them other names.

437 Tempera.

438 Nero. Claudius Caesar Nero (AD 37–68).

439 Scapa Flow In the Orkney Islands.

440 Franz Peter Schubert.

Old Time Music Hall

441 1921. For many years before his death he was seriously ill and his act would frequently be interupted by fits of coughing.

442 He was a chimney sweep, and his real name was Charles Vagg. Three years before his death in 1865, he opened a music hall in Islington and his name survived with it for about a hundred years.

443 James Fawn. Songs about policemen were particularly popular in the second half of the nineteenth century and this one was Fawn's most successful song.

444 1963. An excellent impression of a performance at the Metropolitan can be heard on the Pye record, *Max at the Met* (GGL 0195).

445 Malcolm Scott. Scott began as an actor on the legitimate stage but took to the halls in 1903. He portrayed historical characters – Boadicea, Salomé and the Gibson girl. He was billed as 'The Woman who knows'.

446 1 January 1907. The strike was dramatized in the BBC series, *The Edwardians*, in the programme on Marie Lloyd. The strike lasted about a month.

447 Mrs Ormiston Chant. Mrs Chant was known as one of the 'Prudes on the Prowl', a name coined by the dramatic critic of *The Daily Telegraph*. The LCC decided that the promenade bar and the auditorium should be separated by a partition.

448 Sir Winston Churchill.

449 Harry Fragson. Fragson's father was a Belgian and Harry spoke French and English and performed in both languages, often appearing at the Folies-Bergère. His father shot him in 1903.

450 Nellie Wallace. Nellie Wallace began as a child performer and worked until shortly before her death, aged 78, in 1948. Her recordings – such as that of her song 'Half-past Nine' – evoke, by means of giggles, chuckles, and hiccups, something of her curious figure, with its odd clothes and tatty boa.

451 Belle Elmore, murdered by Dr Crippen. 'Belle Elmore' was Mrs Crippen's stage name. She was not particularly successful and was last seen alive on 31 January 1910. Crippen was hanged on 23 November 1910. His mistress, Ethel Le Neve, was acquitted.

452 Tom Kennedy. Robey was destined for, first the University of Leipzig, and then Cambridge. However his father suffered financial reverses and he had to leave Cambridge and began work as an engineer in Birmingham. A chance visit to Westminster Aquarium led to his volunteering – repeatedly – to be mesmerised by 'Professor' Kennedy.

453 Jack Judge, its part-author, in 1912. Florrie Forde sang it before the War, but revived it in 1914, when it became a hit.

454 Victoria Monks. Two of her songs are especially well-remembered: 'Won't you come home Bill Bailey' and 'Give my regards to Leicester Square'.

455 Granville Bantock under the name 'Graban'. Bantock succeeded Elgar as Professor of Music, University of Birmingham. The show was called 'The A.B.C. Girl' or 'Flossie the Frivolous'.

456 Alec Hurley. Hurley, a coster comic and singer, was Marie Lloyd's second husband.

457 The New Canterbury (by George Augustus Sala). Charles Morton, known as 'The Father of the Halls' opened the Canterbury Hall in 1851 behind the Canterbury Arms Tavern, Westminster Bridge Road, Lambeth. It was enlarged in 1854 and reopened as the New Canterbury Music Hall.

458 Herbert Campbell. 1878 was the year of the patriotic song, 'By Jingo' which the great Macdermott sang. He referred to the Russo-Turkish war and in its chorus had the words: 'and while we're Britons true, the Russians shall not have Constantinople'. Campbell's parody revived both the sentiments.

459 The Wheatsheaf, a public house with a built-on hall. The proprietor was called Balmbra and his name occurs in the song (as does the date, 1862). Three years later the Wheatsheaf became the Oxford Music Hall. The name Balmbra has survived to this day however.

460 Building Societies, Hunting, parody of *Minstrel Boy*. According to the *Daily Telegraph* of 28 November 1901, the choice of songs was left to Leno. He 'first gave his latest one in which he describes his entanglement with a 'building society' and the sort of home he got by going to one'. He followed this with his experiences as a huntsman and then 'as a final effort criticised very freely the *Minstrel Boy*.'

Chemistry

461 The Law of Octaves (an early classification of the elements into groups of eight).

462 Germanium.

463 Prometheum.

464 Lanthanides.

465 They are elements with similar outer electronic structures. They differ in the inner electron shells.

466 Naturally occurring carbon consists of a mixture of isotopes/carbon 12 with (1%) carbon 13.

467 Yes, a mole is just a number. A mole is the amount that contains the same number of entities as there are atoms of carbon 12 in 0·012 kilograms of carbon 12.

468 6×10^{23} (to be precise $6·022169 \times 10^{23}$).

469 The reaction is exothermic.

470 The enthalpy change for an exothermic reaction is negative.

471 Barium – it is:
(a) an alkaline earth metal whereas the others are alkali metals
(b) it is in group 2 of the Periodic Table, the others are in group 1.

472 They are all:
(a) inorganic complexes
(b) complex ions
(c) complexes containing metals linked to non-metal groups.

473 It consists of two interlocked face centred cubes. One face centred cube of sodium ions, one of chloride ions.

474 By electrolysis of molten sodium hydroxide by Sir Humphrey Davey.

475 (a) Delocalization of electrons
(b) Resonance between (valence bond) structures.

476 Two substances, they are:
(a) mirror images
(b) optical isomers.

477 Solutions of the compounds rotate the plane of plane polarized light in opposite directions.

478 (a) Bromine adds to the double bond of hexene
(b) Hexene contains a double bond
(c) Hexene is an olefin.

479 10^{-7}mole per litre. The clue is pH_7.

480 In solution in water very few of the molecules dissociate to hydrogen ions and acetate ions. The strength has nothing to do with the concentration. There is an equilibrium between undissociated acetic acid and the hydrogen ions and acetate ions and this equilibrium favours the molecule acetic acid.

History of the English Language

481 Earth.

482 F.

483 From the time of the first Anglo-Saxon settlements in England to about 1100.

484 Water.

485 The plural form of a noun which is made from the singular by changing the main vowel instead of by adding es or s. There are seven: foot, goose, tooth, man, woman, louse and mouse.

486 The word comes from the Anglo-Saxon or Old English word *dun* meaning hill.

487 Erse (originally the Scottish variant for Irish).

488 Italian.

489 Arabic or Turkish (Arabic *gahwah*, in Turkish pronounced *kahveh*).

490 From Captain Charles Boycott, a land agent who in 1880 was so harsh with the tenants of the Irish Estate of Lord Erne that people refused to have anything to do with him.

491 Celtic Irish – *uisque beatha, usque baugh* – water of life. As 'of life' has been dropped, whisky means water.

492 Light green and leaf (Chlos=light green, and phyllon=leaf).

493 And – per se – and (per se=by itself so the phrase is And-by itself-and).

494 Sir Walter Scott.

495 Great Vowel Shift.

496 From the Latin *audire* to hear and then the French *oir oyer* (modern French ouir)=hear ye.

497 Æ made by combining A and E (known as *ash*).

498 English was spoken and read by only a small nation. Latin was used by many nations as it was the international language of that time. Bacon felt that his work 'would live and be a citizen of the the world' as English books could not.

499 The Danes introduced 'by' into English. It stands for 'village' so by-law means village or local law (law also has a Danish derivation).

500 Cowcumber.

501 Berchtesgaden.

502 Sir Francis Beaufort (1774–1857). The Beaufort Wind Scale. The numbers 0–12 were used as a scale of wind strength in 1806. Force 12 was 'that which no canvas could withstand'.

503 Ferdinand Magellan. He was trying to find a route to the Spice Islands.

504 Peter Ustinov.

505 Vedas.

506 Plimsoll Line. Samuel Plimsoll was MP for Derby.

507 River Tay

508 St Edward's Crown (made for Charles II's Coronation 1662), The Imperial State Crown (made for Victoria 1838), and The Imperial Crown of India (made for the ceremony of crowning King George V as Emperor of India).

509 The Royal Society. Full title – Royal Society of London for Improving Natural Knowledge. First charter passed 15 July 1662, followed by other charters in 1663 and 1669. Newton was President and was re-elected annually until his death in 1727.

510 Edward II. Became first 'English' Prince of Wales. Murdered in Berkeley Castle.

511 The titles were: The Gnome, The Old Castle, Tuileries, Bydlo, Ballet of the Unhatched Chickens, Samuel Goldenburg and Schmuyle, Market Place at Limoges, Catacombs, Baba-Jaga, Great Gate of Kiev.

512 William Shakespeare.

513 Henrik Ibsen.

514 El Greco.

515 First walk in space. From Voskhod II on 18 Marsh 1965. His co-pilot was Belyayev.

516 The Three Fates.

517 Charles the Great (742–814) also known as Charlemagne.

518 Swans. The birds are identified by notches cut on the beak. From the thirteenth to the eighteenth century they were regarded as property of the Crown. The process of marking is called 'swan upping' or 'hopping'.

519 Tycho Brahe.

520 Edward Elgar.

Sea and Ships

521 Five only – the bell, man, foot, bolt and buoy ropes. All the others have special names such as halliards, clewlines, buntlines, sheets, downhauls etc.

522 He was better known as Joseph Conrad. Born in Poland, he became a British shipmaster then a writer.

523 *Pelican* – renamed the *Golden Hind* later.

524 The cook, because he was expected to do the primitive 'doctoring' before this was made a responsibility of the master.

525 None. She made several very fast passages but her rival *Thermopylae* made two 60-day passages from London to Melbourne. The *Cutty Sark*'s best was 64 days land to land on this run. The *Thermopylae* made a run of 91 days Foochow to London in the tea trade which the *Cutty Sark* never approached. (The *Lightning* sailed from Melbourne to Liverpool in 63 days in 1853 – the record.)

526 The *Sirius* in 1838 seems to have been the first Atlantic 'liner' as she crossed using engines as main power throughout. The *Savannah* of 1819 was a sailing-ship which could rig and use briefly a pair of power-driven paddles.

527 Since June 1967.

528 *Nautilus*, an American submarine.

529 Challenger Deep in the Mariana's Trench in the Pacific; depth 36,198 ft.

530 Over 70%.

531 She was the first all-iron sailing ship (the first iron steamship, *Aaron Manby*, was also British).

532 *Savannah* – an American vessel.

533 *Great Britain*.

534 The Apollo 15 spaceship was named *Endeavour* in Cook's honour and carried a piece of the original ship.

535 All three are missing ships, which sailed and disappeared. (The *Waratah* with cargo and passengers, the *Admiral Karpfanger*, a German four-masted barque training ship went missing on a grain passage from Australia, the *Sao Paulo* missing without trace in the Atlantic when being towed to Europe to be scrapped.)

536 A compass slung overhead for the Ship's Master to note the course (and steering skill) when below; it was in his saloon.

537 One which carried no permanent royals.

538 Construct the model outside the bottle first, with hinged masts and collapsible rigging. Then set her in carefully and haul up the rigging by means of ends left trailing through the bottle's neck.

539 His surveying in Newfoundland waters and the St Lawrence River brought him to favourable notice. He was used to ships like the Whitby 'Cat' *Endeavour;* most naval officers were not. (Very probably, senior officers did not want the job. It was Cook who made the expedition important. It could have been simply a passage to and from Tahiti.)

540 The Frenchman Louis De Bougainville.

Medical Science

541 Electrocardiogram.

542 5–6 litres. 5–10% of the body weight or approximately 70 ml/kg or 2500–2800 ml/square metre body surface area.

543 Secondary haemorrhage.

544 The Tidal Volume.

545 A hormone released from the stomach which increases the acidity of the gastric juice. Released from the pyloric antrum. A polypeptide made up of amino acids ending with phenylalanine. Two varieties have been discovered.

546 The Clostridia.

547 Shick test.

548 Seeing in the dark (night vision).

549 Micelles.

550 A second graft from the same donor is rejected more rapidly than the first.

551 Serotonin (5-hydroxytryptamine).

552 The presence of lysozyme (antibacterial enzyme), in the saliva.

553 Vitamin B12 (cyano cobalamin). Vitamin K2 synthesised by intestinal bacteria. It is usually isolated from putrid fishmeal.

554 The well-known sounds which are heard with the stethoscope over an artery when taking (measuring) the blood pressure.

555 Giant pyramidal cells situated in the motor cortex of the brain. Betz was a Russian anatomist who lived about 1850.

556 It is the unit of absorbed dose of radioactivity related to the biological effect – in the therapeutic range 1 roentgen=0·97 rads so the dose in roentgens is roughly equal to the number of rads.

557 Any type of immune response – a recall or redevelopment of antibodies in the blood which had previously been present but had disappeared.

558 A period after a muscle contraction in which no stimulus can produce another contraction.

559 Temporary persistence of a reflex muscle contraction after the stimulus has been withdrawn.

560 Kinins (they increase capillary permeability).

Antiques

561 Mahogany.

562 Porcelain is translucent, pottery does not transmit light.

563 St Louis.

564 ·925 (92·5%).

565 Sheffield Plate.

566 Shagreen.

567 Stump work.

568 Liberty.

569 The Barberini vase.

570 Adam and Sheraton who were not practical cabinet makers (or Chippendale and Hepplewhite because they were practical cabinet makers).

571 Holly.

572 Plymouth and Bristol.

573 Kingwood and Tulipwood.

574 The fashion for painting edges of books with heraldic devices and scenes.

575 Lantern.

576 Painted figures on wood (men – women – housemaids etc) standing about Georgian houses.

577 William Pegg *or* William 'Quaker' Pegg.

578 Gouache.

579 A small table with drawer, having a loose movable bookstand with curved handle and drawers on top.

580 Nonsuch (the name of a palace built by Henry VIII at Cheam, Surrey).

581 The Statue of Liberty. Now to be seen in New York harbour. Its full title was originally 'Liberty Enlightening the World'. It is constructed of ⅛″ hammered copper on a steel frame and weighs 225 tons.

582 Poilus. Derived from 'poilu' meaning hairy, because of their beards.

583 Pogroms. A Russian word, meaning 'destruction' or 'riot'. The Russian central Government did not organise pograms, as was widely believed, but the anti-Semite policy that it carried out from 1881–1917 made them possible. Pogrom has come to mean an attack against a minority (religious, racial, or class) which is either approved or condoned by the authorities.

584 Scapula.

585 Captain Nemo in *Twenty Thousand Leagues Under the Sea* by Jules Verne.

586 Pilgrim Fathers of *The Mayflower*, in December 1620.

587 General Grivas.

588 The Royal Scots. A name given in 1633 by one of the senior French regiments.

589 Jerome K. Jerome (1859–1927).

590 Soldiers of Destiny.

591 Luther's 95 Theses against the Papal Legate.

592 Figures of horses carved on slopes of chalk hills, at Westbury, Wiltshire, and Uffington, Berkshire.

593 John Keats. Sonnet to Fanny Brawne.

594 Arnold Wesker.

595 Lourdes, in France, at the Grotto of Massabielle. Miraculous healings have been claimed from a spring which arose near the site of Bernadette's vision of Mary.

596 Judy Garland.

597 The Duke of Wellington (1796–1852).

598 Galileo.

599 Japanese suicide-pilots. Means literally 'Divine Wind'.

600 Bathsheba.

Gardening

601 The art of training and cutting plants into ornamental shapes.

602 Anther (anther and filament make up the stamen).

603 Soilless gardening.

604 The tip of an unflowered shoot of pink or carnation which can be pulled out and rooted like a cutting.

605 Club root.

606 Cut it hard back to the third or fourth outwardly-pointing bud from the base.

607 Not below $\frac{1}{2}$ inch.

608 A numerical scale on which is measured the degree of acidity or alkalinity of the soil. (Neutral is ph 7 and in scientific terms it is the negative of the number of hydroxyl ions per unit volume of soil).

609 The degree of fineness of the soil particles or crumbs. Thus a good tilth means there are no big lumps in the soil.

610 In spring or early summer.

611 Capability Lancelot Brown (1715–1783).

612 Dwarfing trees, perfected by Japanese gardeners.

613 Cuckoo spit.

614 Shortening the stem of a variety of orange by taking a piece out of the centre and grafting the top back on the base.

615 Erica Cinerea.

616 Saintpaulia.

617 That it is not attacked by or susceptible to wart disease (Black Scab) caused by synchytrium endobioticum.

618 An apple stock. Malling Merton 106 is a semi-dwarfing stock immune to woolly aphis.

619 Crown bud.

620 34 chromosomes. Pitmaston is a triploid pear
(3×17) while Louise is a diploid ($2 \times 17 = 34$).

Mammals

621 The reindeer – called caribou in America.

622 Bats, hedgehogs, dormouse (not squirrel or
badger).

623 The mother licks a wet strip in her fur and the
baby crawls along it to her pouch.

624 Because it curls the end of its prehensile tail into a
ring (not because it is marked with rings).

625 The hippopotamus, which exudes a reddish sticky
sweat that turns brownish on drying and protects
the skin from sun-burn.

626 Either (a) Sea otter, which uses a stone held on
chest as an anvil for cracking sea-urchins; or
(b) Chimpanzee, which uses twigs to fish white
ants out of their nests.

627 The soft palate, blown out with air.

628 The South American rabbit (Sylvilagus), in which
it produces only a mild disease.

629 The American shrew (Blairna), (also European
water-shrew (Neomys), the Solenodon of Cuba and
Hispaniola).

630 The ratel or honey-badger (Mellivora). The bird
calls and flies ahead leading it to a bees' nest.

631 The polar-bear, which stores excess vitamin A
from its vitamin-rich diet in its liver.

632 By resonance in the throat-pouches under the skin
of the neck and chest.

633 Hedgehogs (the prickly Hedgehog-Tenrecs of
Madagascar).

634 Eel grass (Zostera) and similar flowing plants (not
seaweeds or algae).

635 The female gelada baboon – a line of swellings like
beads from neck onto chest.

636 Fisherman bats (Noctilio) of Caribbean; Pizonyx
of Lower California.

637   They trawl for small fish near the surface with their large hind feet with long toes and claws.

638   The eland (in south Africa and at Askania Nova in the Crimea).

639   It is thought to be a sort of acoustic lens to focus sonar ultrasonic sounds in echo-location.

640   The sloths of South America – sometimes as low as 24°C.

General Knowledge 10

641   Cohort.

642   Charles Mason and Jeremiah Dixon. The line is called the Mason Dixon Line.

643   Fruit flies.

644   At Berkeley Castle, Gloucestershire. He was murdered there in 1327.

645   When Charles I attempted to arrest five MP's in the Commons in 1642.

646   Parnassus. Also sacred to Dionysus.

647   Nadir. The pole vertically below the observer's feet.

648   Sir Rowland Hill (in 1840).

649   *Hôtel Des Invalides.*

650   George Washington.

651   Octavian and Antony.

652   The seven kingdoms into which Anglo-Saxon England was divided before AD 900. They were, East Anglia, Essex, Kent, Mercia, Northumbria, Wessex, and Sussex. From the Greek 'rule of seven'.

653   Karlheinz Stockhausen. Born 1928.

654   Slieve Donard. 2,796 ft high, in the Mountains of Mourne. Carrantuohill in the Republic of Ireland is higher.

655   *Iolanthe* by Gilbert and Sullivan.

656   He was drowned – lost in the cruiser *Hampshire* off the Orkneys in 1916. The cruiser was struck by a mine on the passage to North Russia.

657   Pavlov. (Ivan Petrovich).

658   Baseball. The 'bull-pen': an area off the field where substitutes can warm up. 'Strike-out': is three strikes and counts as an out.

659   Chromosomes.

660   Einstein's Theory of Relativity.

Scandinavian Mythology

661   Skirnismal.

662   Freyja.

663   A star.

664   Heimdall.

665   Gold.

666   Thor.

667   Sjaelland (Zealand) and Malaren (old name: Logurinn).

668   Vanir.

669   Edda (Snorri Sturluson c. 1220).

670   A ship.

671   Austri is one of the four dwarves supposed each to support a corner of the heavens.

672   Nerthus in Tacitus: Njord (Njorthur) in Norse sources.

673   Fishing for the Midgard Serpent. (World Serpent, *Mithgarthsorm* [ur] or *Jormungand* [ur]).

674   Ragnarok 'doom of the gods'.

675   The drowning of all the giants save one in Ymir's blood.

676   The fetter, Gleipnir.

677   They said he had choked in his wisdom because nobody there was wise enough to be able to ask him questions.

678   He governed thunder and thunderbolts, winds and rainstorms, fair weather and the fruits of the earth, they invoked him in times of famine and disease.

679 Odin's (Othin's) self-immolation; Odin (Othinn) as all-father Bald(u)r as innocent victim; ideas of punishment and reward in after life; doomsday conceptions.

680 Gods of fertility and prosperity; Njord (Njorthur), Frey (Freyr).

Scottish History

681 Chevy Chase (1388).

682 Catherine Douglas (Barlass) (in an attempt to save King James the first).

683 Devorgilla, daughter of Lord of Galloway, wife of John de Baliol (1250–1313), completed both in memory of her husband.

684 The slaying of the guest involved.

685 1719, at the Battle of Glensheil.

686 Mary MacGregor of Comar (not Helen, as Scott called her).

687 Robert and Edward Bruce in the thirteenth century (Edward was King of Ireland).

688 Simon, Lord Lovat (in 1746, the island was in Loch Morat).

689 *L'Heureux*.

690 They were hereditary custodians of specially precious Celtic saints' relics.

691 Blank papers signed by the Catholic Earls of Huntley, Erroll and Angus for the King of Spain to fill in his own terms for the invasion of Scotland, 1592–93.

692 An offer to return the Stone of Destiny (or scone) – probably because it was not the genuine article.

693 The Gowrie Conspiracy (in 1660).

694 A farcical engagement between the Covenanters and Gordons (in 1639).

695 A shoulder-brooch torn from Bruce with his plaid at Battle of Dal Righ. (Torn off by a MacDougall clansman and retained as a precious trophy by that Clan.)

696 Alexander, Earl of Mar.

697 Bernard De Linton, Abbot of Arbroath.

698 At Garmouth, Moray (on his abortive landing in Scotland, 1650).

699 A game of medieval Scotland, enjoyed particularly by King James V and his Court, consisting of tobogganing on an ox skull.

700 Robert Bruce and John Comyn the Red.

First World War

701 1915 (chlorine gas on 22 April).

702 The Hindenburg Line.

703 They were members of the BEF, and the name comes from an Imperial Order issued by the Germans: 'to walk over General French's contemptible little army'.

704 Austria declared war on Serbia. (Austria declared war on Germany, 4 August, and on Britain, 12 August.)

705 Heligoland.

706 At the Battle of Tannenberg and the Mazurian Lakes.

707 King Constantine of Greece.

708 RFC aircraft. Single-seater biplane scouts.

709 Yarmouth and King's Lynn (L3 and L4 on 19 January 1915).

710 Russian and Austro-Hungarian (Russians won the battle, September and October 1914).

711 The Schlieffen Plan, prepared by Count Alfred von Schlieffen, former chief of general staff. German armies would first crush France in a great fan-like drive through neutral Belgium, then crush Russia, Great Britain, the Balkans and Asia.

712 Enver Pasha.

713 The Kaiser, through his Chancellor.

714 To save Salonika from the enemy, and from the Bulgarians in particular, and to impose an obstacle to Germany's efforts to effect a junction by the most direct route with Turkey.

715 Off the Falkland Islands.

716 Gallipoli Peninsula (Dardanelles). These were the chosen landing sites.

717 The Canadians.

718 Battle of Cambrai, 1917.

719 Marshall Ferdinand Foch, appointed at Doullen 1918.

720 China. Kiau-Chan (Harbour Tsing-Tau).

General Knowledge 11

721 A giant hero of immense drinking and eating capacity.

722 The Tolpuddle Martyrs. Sentenced in 1834 for administering unlawful oaths for seditious purposes at Tolpuddle in Dorset.

723 A Viking Boat. This takes place on the island of Shetland. Held on the last Tuesday in January to welcome the return of the sun. It is a survival of pagan sun worship in which a Viking ship is carried in procession by torchbearers.

724 Californian Gold Rush.

725 *Elements* by Euclid. Said to have a greater circulation than any book in history except the Bible.

726 Hector Hugh Munro (1870–1916). Writer of satirical short stories and novels.

727 Edict of Nantes.

728 Cats eyes. Invented in 1934.

729 Titus Oates. In 1678 Oates revealed an alleged 'popish plot' to kill the King (Charles II) and put his brother James on the throne in order to restore Catholicism.

730 Zero Energy Thermonuclear Assembly. Devised in 1957 by British physicists at Harwell in an attempt to create electrical energy directly from nuclear fusion.

731 Pandora.

732 Jupiter, in Holst's *Planet Suite*.

733 To impress (recruit) men into naval service.

734 Access to the Baltic. The corridor was ten miles wide and 100 miles long, it contained the Port of Danzig.

735 *Pilgrim's Progress*. Written by John Bunyan in 1675.

736 Catherine of Aragon. First wife of Henry VIII, previously the wife of Arthur his elder brother.

737 The Bayeux Tapestry. The tapestry of Queen Matilda – wife of William the Conqueror. Believed to have been made by her.

738 Retiarius.

739 She was the first woman to swim the English Channel, on 6 August 1926.

740 Lorenzo De'Medici (the Magnificent). He ruled with Giuliano De'Medici until 1478, and then alone until 1492.

Poetry

741 A 'Dirty British coaster' (John Masefield's *Cargoes*).

742 *Lyrical Ballads*. Compiled by William Wordsworth and Samuel Taylor Coleridge and published in 1798.

743 My bonnie Mary (the title of the poem; 'Go fetch to me a pint o' wine').

744 The Ettrick Shepherd.

745 The cuckoo (in *To the Cuckoo*).

746 Dylan Thomas (in *Fern Hill*).

747 Father and son (Rustum the father, and Sohrab the son in *Sohrab and Rustum*).

748 Hugh McDiarmid.

749 The mountain lion. (The title of the poem. The animal is sometimes called a puma.)

750 The Franklin.

751 *Epithalamion*. Published at the same time were the *Amoretti*, a cycle of sonnets commemorative of his moods in courtship. They did not celebrate his wedding. *Prothalamion* describes himself as a disappointed suitor at court.

752 'Here he lies where he longed to be; Home is the sailor, Home from the sea; and the Hunter, home from the hill'.

753 East Coker.

754 *Marmion*

755 'Earth has not anything to show more fair'.

756 In the Claypit. (Title: *Christ in the Claypit*.)

757 Auburn.

758 'My three and twentieth year.' (Title: *How soon hath time, the subtle thief of youth*.)

759 'On first looking into Chapman's Homer' (title of the sonnet).

760 Henry Reed.

Astronomy 2

761 Carbon dioxide.

762 Astronomer Royal (of England – Scotland has her own).

763 The fall of the Tunguska Meteorite.

764 Aristarchus.

765 Vulcan.

766 Arcturus. (Sirius, Canopus and Alpha Centauri are all brighter, but lie south of the equator. Arcturus is very slightly brighter than Capella and Vega.)

767 Sir Richard Woolley.

768 Halley's Comet.

769 Sigma Octantis.

770 Auriga, The Charioteer or Wagoner.

771 Oberon.

772 Jack Bennett.

773 In the Pleiades (in Taurus).

774 Ceres.

775 Gregorian.

776 George Alcock.

777 Wilhelm Beer.

778 Mare Imbrium.

779 O-type.

780 John G. Bolton and Gordon J. Stanley.

French Literature

781 Harpagon.

782 Lamartine. (In 1816, at the age of 26, he met a young married woman, Julie Charles, at Aix-les-Bains, on the Lac du Bourget; they planned to meet again the following year, but Mme Charles was then too ill to travel and died shortly afterwards of tuberculosis. In 1820 Lamartine published a short book of poems, *Méditations poétiques*, in memory of their idyll. It was the first book of Romantic poetry to be published in France.)

783 *Les Plaideurs* – 1668 (the play is very freely based on Aristophanes, and is a satire on the French law courts and on the mania of private persons for going to law).

784 Julien Sorel, a passionately ambitious young man who chose the black robe of the priest rather than the red uniform of the soldier to make his way up the ladder.

785 Ferney – now Ferney-Voltaire. He chose to live near the border between Geneva and France so that he could cross the frontier whenever persecution by either the Genevan or the French authorities seemed likely.

786 *L'invitation au Château* (1947).

787 Prosper Mérimée, 1803–70. His story was written in 1845. Mérimée was a civil servant who for some time held the post of Inspector of Ancient Monuments.

788 Etienne Martin. A young student who lives with his mother in a small Paris apartment.

789 *Les Iambes*. (Chenier was executed in 1794, during the Terror, at the age of 32. *Les Iambes*, however, were not published until 1919, when they immediately aroused great interest among the young Romantic poets. The theme of these poems was political satire, coupled with lamentations on his own fate.)

790 Angoulême, some 300 miles south-west of Paris. (From Angoulême, Lucien Chardon – later known as Lucien de Rubempre – set out to seek fame and fortune in Paris.)

791 Jean-Paul Sartre, the leader of the Existentialist Movement.

792 *Les Thibault* (eleven volumes were written between 1922 and 1940).

793 Pléiade.

794 *Thérèse Desqueyroux*, 1927 (by François Mauriac, one of his best and possibly most characteristic novels).

795 *L'Espoir*, 1937. (Malraux was an organiser and pilot of the Republican Air Force. Politician, man of letters and art historian, André Malraux was for several years Minister for Cultural Affairs under General de Gaulle.)

796 The Cévennes, which form the eastern part of the massif central.

797 Clément Marot. His poem *L'Enfer* was written after this experience, and is topically interesting in these days of political persecution.

798 *Perceval* by Chrétien de Troyes. (This verse romance, written in the 1180s and left incomplete on the poet's death, introduces the myth of the Grail into the Arthurian legend.)

799 Roger Caillois, who was elected to the Académie Française in 1971. (His work, *Pierres*, was published in 1966. Roger Caillois combines literature with a career in administration – he holds an important post at UNESCO in Paris.)

800 Jean de Meung, who added some 18,000 lines to the 4,000 written by his predecessor. (This long poem was the most popular single work of the thirteenth century.)

General Knowledge 12

801 Lord Nelson. Destroyed 8 March 1966.

802 Daedalus.

803 Tobias Smollett.

804 A marriage union between one of royal or noble rank and one of lower rank in which the wife does not acquire the husband's rank and the offspring do not inherit the titles or possessions of the father.

805 Lord Have Mercy.

806 Tonic Sol-fa. Established and perfected by John Curwen (d. 1863).

807 The Verrazano-narrows bridge. Opened in 1964.

808 Vienna, in 1923. The Central Radio Station for this organisation is centred near Paris.

809 The Fosse Way. One of the principal Roman roads of Britain. It runs on the line: Axmouth-Ilchester-Bath-Cirencester-Leicester-Lincoln. The name derives from the Latin for ditch (*fosse*) which ran on each side of the road.

810 Three. *Bounty*, 1789; *Nore*, 1797; *Australia*, 1808.

811 From the Greek legend of the mortal Arachne who challenged the gods to surpass her at weaving. She failed and was turned into a spider by Minerva.

812 Daphne Jackson, Surrey University.

813 Prokofiev.

814 Ptolemy I.

815 The Friendly Islands. The king's full name is King Taufa'ahau Tupou IV of Tonga.

816 Botticelli (Sandro di) (1444/5–1510). Properly Alessandro Di Marian or Di Vanni Filipepi.

817 A district, parish, church, or deanery of the Church of England which lies under the jurisdiction of the Crown and not of the Bishop of the Diocese in which it is situated. Included are the Chapel Royal, St James' Palace, London, and St George's Chapel in Windsor Castle.

818 The area was returned to Germany. It had been ceded to France after the First World War under the supervision of the League of Nations.

819 Simone de Beauvoir. She won the Goncourt Prize in 1954.

820 Lollards. Lollardy, a Medieval English movement for ecclesiastical reform. Led by John Wycliffe whose 'poor priests' spread his ideas throughout the countryside in the late fourteenth century.

Science Fiction

821 Ray Bradbury's *Fahrenheit 451* (the hero's name is Guy Montag).

822 The Plan was to establish two centres of learning at opposite ends of the galaxy, to promote Civilisation after the fall of the galactic empire as predicted by the psycho-historian Hari Seldon (by Isaac Asimov).

823 *The Space Machine* by Frederick Pohl and C. M. Kornbluth (earlier title in the USA was *Gravy Planet*).

824 Dr Wellington Yueh (in Frank Herbert's *Dune*).

825 Ride it. It is an eight-legged beast of burden. (Character created by Edgar Rice Burroughs.)

826 Robert A. Heinlein's *Blow Ups Happen*.

827 They are all set in 'Generation Starships', Spaceships designed to travel for centuries while supporting an entirely self-sufficient population.

828 The Quest for the Holy Grail (much is made of the Tarot pack, but this is of course subsidiary).

829 Make him take his hat off, or possibly pull his hair. The mind-reading powers of true Slans are governed by golden tendrils growing among the hair (*Slan* by A. E. van Vogt).

830 The 'Spindizzy' drive, enabling ships and worlds to travel faster than light.

831 The Heat Ray, the poisonous black smoke, the three-legged fighting machines, the multi-legged crab-like handling machines. (Also mentioned are three cylindrical spaceships and the Red Weed.)

832 It was a dot, a single dot, which means in Tralfamadorian: 'Greetings' (in Kurt Vonnegut's *The Sirens of Titan*).

833 *Tiger! Tiger!* by Alfred Bester. (Earlier title, *The Stars My Destination*. Its hero is Gulliver or Gully Foyle alias Fonrmile of Ceres.)

834 Venus, or Perelandra, where Ransom fought the Un-Man (C. S. Lewis's *Out of the Silent Planet* trilogy).

835 Courage. All sane puppeteers are cowards (Larry Niven's *Neutron Star* and *Ringworld*).

836 Arthur C. Clarke's *2001*.

837 A robot may not injure a human being, or, through inaction, allow a human being to come to harm. (The second law was: A robot must obey the orders given it by human beings except where such orders would conflict with the first law; the third law was: A robot must protect its own existence as long as such protection does not conflict with the First or Second laws.)

838 J. G. Ballard.

839 The 'Players' are, on the one side, hostile amorphous entities who prey on planoforming spaceships; and on the other, telepathically linked pairs of cats and human sensitives (*The Game of Rat and Dragon* by Cordwainer Smith a pen-name for Paul T. Linebarger).

840 Attel Malagate (the Woe), Viole Falushe, Kokor Hekkus (the killing machine), Howard Alan Treesong, Lens Larque. (Vance has already produced novels about the first three, respectively, *Star King*, *The Temple of Love* and *The Killing Machine*.)

Spanish and South American Ethnology

841 Prince Juan Carlos Bourbon.

842 El Greco.

843 Tango.

844 The northern coast of South America.

845 Over the issue of the liberation of Cuba.

846 Hermando de Soto.

847 Gibraltar was one of them, and the other, Ceuta stood across the Straits of Gibraltar on the African coast.

848 Rio de Janeiro, Brazil.

849 Treaty of Utrecht, 1713.

850 Poem of the Cid. *El Cid* written about 1140.
Real name of El Cid, a Spanish national hero, Rodrigo Diaz.

851 A mixture of sorrowful Indian and joyous Spanish music (native American).

852 The wheel.

853 Llamas and Alpacas. Guanacos and vicunas run wild and were hunted by them.

854 The Sacred Book of the Quiche Maya Indians who lived in Central America. The original is now lost, but it survived in oral tradition and was rewritten in Latin characters in the middle of the sixteenth century.

855 A stone column (or stele) found at Tres Zapotes (one of the centres of Olmec culture) bearing a hieroglyphic date corresponding to the year 31 BC.

856 Tiahuanaco is in the south Bolivian highlands near Lake Titicaca. Around AD 500 it was the ceremonial centre of unknown Indians with an advanced culture, as is attested by the imposing stonework ruins which were left after their conquest by the Incas.

857 Quetzalcoatl.

858 Quechua.

859 The names given to the two co-rulers of the chibcha Indians (Colombia). The Zipa controlled the lands around modern Bogota, and the Zaque the district around Tunja.

860 They were the Gods of Ancient Mexico. (Xochipilli, depicted as a young god of maize, was the god of vegetation, games, singing and dancing; Huitzilopochtli, who appeared as a humming bird, was the chief tribal god who demanded to be fed on human hearts; and Tlaloc, a serpent, was the rain god and guardian of water.)

Money, Money, Money

861 The House of Fraser.

862 Gladstone.

863 About fourteen pence.

864 Fourty-four countries.

865 Lloyd's of London.

866 Lloyd George, in 1909.

867 American Express.

868 Ricardo (described by Keynes).

869 Say's Law.

870 Barings.

871 1932.

872 The London Stock Exchange.

873 2·60%.

874 1833.

875 Overseas Government Bonds and Railway Securities.

876 One, 1970.

877 John D. Rockefeller, 1929.

878 They doubled.

879 Czarist Russia.

880 65%.

General Knowledge 13

881 Ralph Vaughan Williams.

882 Double Helix (Deoxyribonucleic acid).

883 Rhubarb. The stalk used in cooking and the root in medicine, notably as a purgative.

884 Wilfred Wilson Gibson (1878–1962). A member of the 'Georgian Group', published: *Daily Bread* 1910, *Thoroughfares* 1914, and many other titles.

885 His paintings – he is better known as Canaletto (1697–1768).

886 French Kings. Charles I to V, although Louis VI was also called 'The Fat' and Philip IV was called 'The Fair'.

887 Eva Braun. They married on 29 April 1945 and committed suicide 30 April.

888 Legion of Honour.

889 Sugar Loaf.

890 Le Corbusier (1887–1965). Professional name of Charles Edouard Jeanneret.

891 Georgia.

892 The Siege of Sidney Street. Churchill was Home Secretary at that time.

893 The Three Graces. Their Greek names are Aglaia, Eruprosyme and Thalia. The Three Graces or three charities. Also known as the personification of Beauty, Charm, and Grace; and Brightness, Joyfulness and Bloom.

894 Elizabeth Garrett Anderson.

895 Dr Thomas Augustine Arne, about 1740.

896 Charles VII (1403–1461). Crowned 1429.

897 Golf US Masters Tournament or Golf Augusta Tournament.

898 Alexander the Great. The Oracle foretold that who- ever did this would rule over Asia.

899 Hamilton.

900 Whigs.

Three other quiz books based on BBC programmes.

Quiz Ball

Since 1966, when BBC TV's first QUIZ BALL
programme was shown, the majority of Britain's top
soccer players have had the opportunity of showing their
skill off the field by answering sporting and general
knowledge questions. The book contains hundreds of
questions (and answers) arranged so that Quiz Ball can
be played at home.

30p

Ask The Family 2

For seven years BBC 1's Ask The Family has been one
of the most popular quiz programmes. This selection of
questions and answers will give hours of enjoyment to
every family.

25p

Brain of Britain

For over twenty years a general knowledge quiz written
and devised by John P. Wynn has been a regular feature
on British and overseas radio programmes. This book,
with over eight hundred questions (and their answers)
arranged in subject quizzes, reflects the tremendous
diversity of the programme. It will provide hours of
enjoyment for quiz enthusiasts and for the young and
not-so-young who want to improve their general
knowledge.

35p